NEW DIRECTIONS FOR TEACHING AND LEARNING

Marilla D. Svinicki, *University of Texas, Austin*
EDITOR-IN-CHIEF

R. Eugene Rice, *American Association for Higher Education*
CONSULTING EDITOR

Teaching to Promote Intellectual and Personal Maturity: Incorporating Students' Worldviews and Identities into the Learning Process

Marcia B. Baxter Magolda
Miami University

EDITOR

Number 82, Summer 2000

JOSSEY-BASS PUBLISHERS
San Francisco

TEACHING TO PROMOTE INTELLECTUAL AND PERSONAL MATURITY: INCORPORATING STUDENTS' WORLDVIEWS AND IDENTITIES INTO THE LEARNING PROCESS
Marcia B. Baxter Magolda (ed.)
New Directions for Teaching and Learning, no. 82
Marilla D. Svinicki, Editor-in-Chief
R. Eugene Rice, Consulting Editor

Microfilm copies of issues and articles are available in 16mm and 35mm, as well as microfiche in 105mm, through University Microfilms Inc., 300 North Zeeb Road, Ann Arbor, Michigan 48106-1346.

ISSN 0271-0633   ISBN 0-7879-5446-2

NEW DIRECTIONS FOR TEACHING AND LEARNING is part of The Jossey-Bass Higher and Adult Education Series and is published quarterly by Jossey-Bass Inc., Publishers, 350 Sansome Street, San Francisco, California 94104-1342. Periodicals postage paid at San Francisco, California, and at additional mailing offices. Postmaster: Send address changes to New Directions for Teaching and Learning, Jossey-Bass Inc., Publishers, 350 Sansome Street, San Francisco, California 94104-1342.

New Directions for Teaching and Learning is indexed in College Student Personnel Abstracts, Contents Pages in Education, and Current Index to Journals in Education (ERIC).

SUBSCRIPTIONS cost $58.00 for individuals and $104.00 for institutions, agencies, and libraries. Prices subject to change.

EDITORIAL CORRESPONDENCE should be sent to the editor-in-chief, Marilla D. Svinicki, The Center for Teaching Effectiveness, University of Texas at Austin, Main Building 2200, Austin, TX 78712-1111.

Cover photograph by Richard Blair/Color & Light © 1990.

www.josseybass.com

CONTENTS

About This Publication. Since 1980, *New Directions for Teaching and Learning (NDTL)* has brought a unique blend of theory, research, and practice to leaders in postsecondary education. *NDTL* sourcebooks strive not only for solid substance but also for timeliness, compactness, and accessibility.

The series has four goals: to inform readers about current and future directions in teaching and learning in postsecondary education, to illuminate the context that shapes these new directions, to illustrate these new directions through examples from real settings, and to propose ways in which these new directions can be incorporated into still other settings.

This publication reflects the view that teaching deserves respect as a high form of scholarship. We believe that significant scholarship is conducted not only by researchers who report results of empirical investigations but also by practitioners who share disciplined reflections about teaching. Contributors to *NDTL* approach questions of teaching and learning as seriously as they approach substantive questions in their own disciplines, and they deal not only with pedagogical issues but also with the intellectual and social context in which these issues arise. Authors deal on the one hand with theory and research and on the other with practice, and they translate from research and theory to practice and back again.

About This Volume. This issue focuses on an important variable that influences our success as teachers: the development of our students as individuals. The importance of the contribution of students' worldviews to learning cannot be overstated. The authors in this volume help us to understand that relationship and suggest what we might be able to do in response to it.

MARILLA D. SVINICKI, *editor-in-chief, is director of the Center for Teaching Effectiveness at the University of Texas, Austin.*

R. EUGENE RICE, *consulting editor, is director, Forum on Faculty Roles and Rewards, AAHE.*

EDITOR'S NOTES

Why won't she just tell us what should be in the paper?" a student laments to a friend. "They will not think; they just want the answers handed to them," a professor complains to a colleague. This gap in expectations exists across campuses, across disciplines, for veteran and new teachers, and for talented and not-so-talented students. Students assume that professors who do not clearly the "truth" are incompetent; professors assume that students who want only the answers are poorly prepared or lazy. This volume of *New Directions for Learning and Teaching* offers an alternative diagnosis of this expectations gap: that professors' expectations often go far beyond students' assumptions about the nature of knowledge. Robert Kegan (1994) explains that it is not *what* students think but rather *how* they think that is important in the learning process. Students who believe that knowledge is certain and held by authorities ask those authorities for "the truth," whereas students who believe that knowledge is relative to a context and acquired through inquiry look to professors to guide them in that inquiry process. Thus how students make meaning mediates how they learn. This volume introduces faculty to the multiple dimensions of meaning-making that affect learning, offers ways to engage in dialogue with students to tap into their particular ways of making meaning, and articulates teaching practices that effectively link teaching and students' diverse ways of meaning-making.

This volume takes a holistic view of learning and development (King and Baxter Magolda, 1996). Three assumptions form the core of this view. First, individual learning and knowledge claims are grounded in how individuals construct knowledge. Learners' assumptions about the nature, limits, and certainty of knowledge, referred to as *cognition* or *epistemology,* mediate *how* they learn. Learners interpret their experiences to form assumptions, reorganize those assumptions in the face of new experiences, and use those assumptions to guide meaning-making. Second, how learners construct and use knowledge is closely tied to their sense of self. For example, complex assumptions about knowledge are necessary but insufficient to make wise judgments in a context because a coherent sense of identity that operates outside of approval of others is also required. Learners who are intensely concerned about what others think of them have difficulty authoring their own views. Thus the intrapersonal (sense of self) and interpersonal (relations with others) dimensions mediate the epistemological dimension of development. Third, the process through which learners interpret their experiences improves in a developmentally related fashion over time. Assumptions about the nature of knowledge become more complex with educational experiences, generally moving from assuming that knowledge is certain to assuming that it must be evaluated in a context. Sense of self and relation to others develop over time, generally emerging from definitions dependent on others' approval to definitions of self as interdependent with others. Where learners are on these continua has a dramatic effect on how they approach learning. Promoting student learning requires understanding the multiple dimensions of human development that mediate learning and possible ways in which they evolve through experience.

This volume emphasizes the multiple possibilities through which students make meaning. No single definitive theory describes the developmental pathways of all students. Instead, theories sketch possible patterns of development. Marilyn Frye notes, "Naming patterns is like charting the prevailing winds over a continent, which does not imply that every individual and item in the landscape is identically affected" (1990, p. 180). The theories presented here are patterns that do not affect all students in the same ways. These theories do describe pathways that have been identified for particular students in diverse contexts and may offer possibilities for understanding students beyond the contexts in which the theories were derived. The volume emphasizes understanding possibilities for student meaning-making and dialogue with one's own students to understand their particular ways of making meaning.

Content

Theoretical portraits of students' meaning-making form the core content of this volume. Some theoretical perspectives integrate all three dimensions of development (epistemological, intrapersonal, and interpersonal), while others bring a particular dimension to the forefront. Perspectives are drawn from various groups of learners to illuminate the possibilities posed by gender, race, ethnicity, and sexual orientation. Because all these theoretical perspectives are grounded in particular groups of students, frameworks are offered to help educators engage their own students in dialogue to gain an understanding of the particular development of these students. Authors describe and illustrate the kinds of dialogue that can help students share how they make meaning. Finally, teaching assumptions and practices that help faculty link their teaching to students' ways of learning are explored. The authors link their active inquiry agendas in student development and learning with their perspectives as practicing faculty members.

Organization

In Chapter One, Michael Ignelzi offers a comprehensive view of students' self-evolution based on Robert Kegan's work. All three dimensions of development are audible in these students' narratives and help faculty understand the complexity of students' meaning-making and its implications for learning. The epistemological dimension takes center stage in Chapters Two and Three, where Patricia King and Blythe Clinchy illustrate trajectories of students' view of knowledge and their ability to construct it. Both authors offer specific approaches for promoting intellectual development through linking learning goals to students' views of knowledge and gender-related approaches to learning. Chapter Four brings identity development to the forefront in the form of Robert Rhoads's conceptualization of the caring self—a merger of complex intrapersonal and interpersonal development. Rhoads shares students' journeys in developing caring identities through service learning, highlighting the components that promote the caring self needed for a democratic society.

Chapters Five through Eight explore various facets of identity development, their role in mediating learning, and their implications for creating learning environments that are responsive to diversity. Mary Howard-Hamilton articulates the development of both African American and white racial identity and identifies characteristics of culturally responsive teaching. Sharon Fries-Britt shares the stories of high-ability African American students and the learning environments they encountered that promoted their racial identity development and learning simultaneously. Anna Ortiz explains ethnic identity development, the cognitive dimension of racial understanding, and the cognitive, intrapersonal, and interpersonal dynamics of intercultural competence. Nancy Evans illustrates the link between students' sexual orientation identity development and learning, highlighting how sexual orientation identity develops and how faculty can create inclusive learning environments that promote gay, lesbian, and bisexual students' learning. In the concluding chapter, I use young adults' stories from a longitudinal project on learning and intellectual development to integrate the various dimensions of development advanced in the first eight chapters. I include a synthesis of recommendations for accessing students' development and principles that the collective authors offer for effective teaching practice. In closing, I would like to thank Michelle Dunn for her generous assistance in editing and proofreading this volume.

Marcia B. Baxter Magolda
Editor

References

Frye, M. "The Possibility of Feminist Theory." In D. L. Rhode (ed.), *Theoretical Perspectives on Sexual Difference*. New Haven, Conn.: Yale University Press, 1990.

Kegan, R. *In Over Our Heads: The Mental Demands of Modern Life*. Cambridge, Mass.: Harvard University Press, 1994.

King, P. M., and Baxter Magolda, M. B. "A Developmental Perspective on Learning." *Journal of College Student Development*, 1996, *37*, 163–173.

MARCIA B. BAXTER MAGOLDA *is professor of educational leadership at Miami University, Oxford, Ohio.*

1

Meaning-making, the process of how individuals make sense of knowledge, experience, relationships, and the self, must be considered in designing college curricular environments supportive of learning and development.

Meaning-Making in the Learning and Teaching Process

Michael Ignelzi

Robert Kegan, whose theory of meaning-making is the focus of this chapter, relates a story told to him by a mother about her preschool-age son. The son, named Johnny, comes to his mother one day and tells her he needs some cow toenails. Living in the suburbs, the mother's first thought is how in the world she will obtain cow toenails, but she is even more intrigued by why her son needs these items. When she asks, Johnny informs her that he is starting a farm and wants to plant the cow toenails to grow some cows. Mom's initial thought is the confirming sense of how inventive and cute her son is. Upon reflection, however, she decides that since Johnny raised the issue, it might be a good time to teach him a little about "the birds and the bees" (or in this case, "the cows"). After telling him a few basic facts about reproduction, she says, "So you see, Johnny, *that* is where baby cows really come from." Johnny, who had been listening intently, pauses for a few moments and then replies, "Not on my farm!"

Children, who tend to be very honest about what they are thinking and feeling as well as what they do and don't understand, often provide clear insights into truisms about how human beings function. Although this volume is dedicated to developmental considerations in the learning and teaching of college students, the story about Johnny illustrates some key developmental principles that are useful in considering how all humans experience and learn:

1. *Humans actively construct their own reality.* William Perry (1970) states that what an organism does is organize and what a human organism organizes is meaning. Kegan (1982, 1994) calls this process *meaning-making.*

Clearly, Johnny and his mother are making meaning in qualitatively different ways. In a sense, their understanding of reality resides on different "farms." We seem intuitively to understand that children and adults construct reality somewhat differently; however, we may not fully appreciate the extent to which adults can also make meaning in qualitatively different ways from each other.

2. *Meaning-making develops over time and experience.* Much of the reason Johnny and his mother construct their understanding of reality in different ways is due to their being at different points in their individual meaning-making development. Kegan views meaning-making as a process that continues to develop throughout one's life span. As Johnny grows and develops, he will move from his current "farm" (way of making-meaning) to new "farms," as may his mother as she continues to gain experience in her adult life.

3. *The process of learning and teaching is strongly influenced by the ways participants make meaning.* New experience and learning are interpreted through our current constructions of reality. When we are presented with information that doesn't fit our meaning-making, as Johnny did, we may discount or ignore it. Continuing to live on our "own farm" where we are comfortable and reasonably secure may at a given time look more desirable than moving to or even visiting that "new farm" down the road. Education isn't simply presenting more adequate information in an effective manner; it is a process that must incorporate the developmental readiness of the student (Johnson and Hooper, 1982) and must construct a developmental "bridge" between the student's current way of understanding and the new way, thus providing a path on which to cross over (Kegan, 1994).

This chapter provides an overview of Robert Kegan's theory of meaning-making development. It describes how individuals' understanding of their experience, of themselves, and of their interpersonal relationships evolves. The focus is on the portion of Kegan's model of self-evolution that describes the developmental transitions individuals face from adolescence through adulthood. Interview data are used to illustrate the theory and how it applies to the college learning and teaching process. Examples are given on how to assess students' developmental levels, along with suggestions on how faculty can support meaning-making development as a means of enhancing student learning.

Robert Kegan's Theory of Meaning-Making

Robert Kegan's theory of meaning-making development is a conceptualization of how human beings make meaning of themselves, of others, and of their experiences throughout the life span. Kegan (1982, 1994), along with other constructive developmental theorists (including Piaget, 1967;

Kohlberg, 1984; Baxter Magolda, 1992; and King and Kitchener, 1994), contends that individuals actively construct their own sense of reality. An event does not have a particular solitary meaning attached that simply gets transferred to the individual. Instead, meaning is created between the event and the individual's reaction to it. Kegan (1982) refers to this as "the zone of mediation"—"the place where the event is privately composed, made sense of, the place where it actually *becomes* an event for that person" (p. 2). This zone where meaning gets made is also referred to by personality psychologists as the self, the ego, or the person. Kegan states: "The activity of being a person is the activity of meaning-making. There is no feeling, no experience, no thought, no perception, independent of a meaning-making context in which it *becomes* a feeling, an experience, a thought, a perception, because we *are* the meaning-making context" (p. 11).

Kegan's theory examines how meaning-making evolves throughout the life span. His developmental approach suggests that the internal structure individuals use to organize meaning-making, and therefore the self, change and evolve in regular and systematic ways. The general course and direction of these changes are predictable over time and experience. Kegan's theory is ambitious in that he proposes that one developmental process (meaning-making) encompasses or accounts for the variety of changes humans go through over the course of their lives pertaining to how they make sense of experience, knowledge, each other, and themselves. Furthermore, he contends that there is consistency in an individual's meaning-making at any particular point in time, such that how one understands knowledge or experience is directly related to how one understands others and the self.

Orders of Consciousness. Kegan proposes a series of six holistic (each with its own internal logic) and qualitatively different forms of meaning-making that individuals may evolve through during their lifetime. He calls these major places along the path of self-evolution "orders of consciousness" and numbers them from 0 to 5 (Kegan, 1994). As a person's development proceeds between and through these orders, meaning-making undergoes changes that affect the person's view of the self, relations to others, and understanding of experience.

Kegan (1994) contends and research on his theory supports that the majority of the adult population (from late adolescence through adulthood) makes meaning at or between order 3 and order 4. The story of adult-meaning-making development seems to be largely described by the slow evolution of the self from order 3 to order 4. As such, it is useful in considering how meaning-making development affects learning and teaching in higher education, to examine the psychological characteristics of these two orders.

Order 3. Order 3 meaning-makers co-construct their sense of meaning with other persons and sources (books, ideas) in their environment. They are not psychologically differentiated from these "co-constructions." That is, the individual's sense of self is based on a *fusion* of others' expectations, theories, and ideas, and those expectations become integrated into how one thinks about oneself. The individual's sense of meaning-making resides partly in other people and sources and partly within the self, so there is no coherent sense of meaning-making or self apart from those other people and sources. An order 3 meaning-maker is masterful at coordinating others' points of view and can create a shared reality with others but is limited in the ability to reflect on that shared reality and how it is influencing or determining the person's own view (Kegan, Noam, and Rogers, 1982). When an order 3 meaning-maker shares what she or he thinks, believes, or feels, another (person or source) is always implicated.

An example of order 3 meaning-making is illustrated by Mike, a graduate student, who discusses the influence of a particular counseling theory on his thinking when working with others (Ignelzi, 1994, p. 133):

> I'm a Rogerian . . . like the Carl Rogers theory, you know. Client-centered theory and things like that. I believe in the empowerment of students and I believe . . . that it's important not to solve student problems but to help them solve problems for themselves. And that deals a lot with some of the theories that we learn in class and, of course, Rogers. So I think about that when dealing with students. I don't really think about it, but I think that those theories have become so much a part of me that they're almost innate, natural. . . . I think that's the framework that I'm in when I deal with students, and whatever style I'm developing, I think it is right off the heels of Rogers.

Mike's meaning-making is reflective of order 3 in that he uncritically adopts a particular theory that has come to guide his thinking and approach in his attempts to help other students. His philosophy, as he describes it, is co-constructed with an external source he accepts wholly without reflection or modification. He defines himself, at least in the counseling context, as fully identified with the Rogerian approach such that his view of himself as a counselor is indistinguishable from that approach.

Order 4. Order 4 meaning-makers construct their sense of meaning and the self such that self-authorship is the key feature. The order 4 individual transcends the co-constructed self of order 3 by developing the ability to differentiate a self-standard apart from, but in relation to, other people and sources. That is, the self can internalize multiple points of view, reflect on them, and construct them into one's own theory about oneself and one's experience. Thus the individual's meaning-making is influenced by but not determined by external sources. The self becomes identified through these self-authored conceptualizations, giving the self an enduring identity that remains fairly stable across contexts and interpersonal relationships.

An example of order 4 meaning-making is illustrated by Amanda, a recent M.A. graduate, who discusses how she is developing her own personal theory about how to make sense and use of theories and concepts she has studied (Ignelzi, 1994, pp. 218–219):

I like to think that there's a framework of some sort, that there are obviously principles and values and different ideas which are part of a lot of different theories that help shape the way I do things and the way I interact with people. I've certainly never been able, you know, not been a person who could even subscribe to one particular theory or theorist and say, "This is it." Because they are all far too limiting, and there are so many that I'm attracted to, and different facets and different things click with me. . . . I think what I liked so much about theory was the process of applying theory, was the whole process of self-discovery with each new theory, that made me, as we talked about a theory, where I had to think about my own life and my own experiences and see, you know, Does this fit? Does this not fit? And I think that it's a process for me, with all the theoretical experiences and like who I've become as a result of that and the different things that I've thought about. That's what I use the most. . . . So I think it's sort of an internalized, you know, inside there's your little self theory.

Amanda's meaning-making is reflective of order 4 in that she is self-authoring her own theory about how to interact with and help others in a counseling context. Though certain formal theories resonate with her more than others do, she reports being attracted to many or parts of many theories. The way she thinks about and uses these theories is highly personalized, based largely on her own values and experiences. Even if many of her ideas are influenced by various theoretical approaches, her understanding, organization, and use of them are determined by her own evolving theory about her work and herself.

"In over Our Heads" in the Learning and Teaching Environment

Given the two different forms of meaning-making (orders 3 and 4) illustrated by Mike and Amanda, it can be postulated that they experience and respond to college learning environments in contrasting ways. While Mike depends on his instructors, course concepts, and peers to co-construct and largely determine what he thinks and believes, Amanda internalizes these same sources to inform and influence (but not determine) her self-authored view. Mike has difficulty with and may not fully understand class assignments that require him to critique or evaluate conflicting perspectives on his own, while Amanda thrives on such learning opportunities. Amanda largely takes responsibility for her own learning, using available resources (professor, reading, peer discussion) in service of her own learning goals. Mike is likely to rely solely on learning goals and standards set by the professor and may hold the professor and others responsible for whether those goals are met. Amanda tends to view criticism of her ideas or work in relation to her own standards, and she ultimately decides their value to her self-authored views of knowledge and self; Mike is much more sensitive to and affected by such constructive criticism because he co-constructs his ideas and sense of self with the same external sources from which the criticism may originate.

It is for these reasons, among others, that Kegan (1994) suggests that many college students may find themselves "in over their heads" in their learning environments. Kegan contends that there is a developmental mismatch between the meaning-making order of most college students—predominantly order 3—and the mental demands of contemporary learning culture—predominantly order 4. Consequently, students like Mike, similar to our preschooler Johnny, are residing on one "farm" while the learning and teaching life of the college are occurring on another.

Kegan reviewed much of the contemporary literature on adult education and found that what is being demanded of students' minds by most education specialists and college faculty requires order 4 meaning-making. Kegan summarized these demands on the mind, which he referred to as the "hidden curriculum," as follows:

- Exercise critical thinking.
- Be a self-directed learner (take initiative; set our own goals and standards; use experts, institutions, and other resources to pursue these goals; take responsibility for our direction and productivity in learning).
- See ourselves as the co-creators of the culture (rather than only shaped by culture).
- Read actively (rather than only receptively) with our own purpose in mind.
- Write to ourselves, and bring our teachers into our self-reflection (rather than write mainly to our teachers and for our teachers).
- Take charge of the concepts and theories of a course or discipline, marshaling on behalf of our independently chosen topic its internal procedures for formulating and validating knowledge [Kegan, 1994, p. 303].

Kegan contends that as curricular aspirations for students to work toward, these goals are important and developmentally sound. In fact, as King and Baxter Magolda (1996) suggest, "The achievement of self-authorship and personal authority should be heralded as a central purpose of higher education" (p. 166). However, when faculty come to expect that all students have order 4 abilities, many students find themselves in a learning environment where they are "in over their heads." Being in over one's head is not a pleasant experience; it is often accompanied by feelings of anxiety, frustration, doubt, and helplessness. These feelings are not conducive to learning.

It is important to note that meaning-making level is not the same as intellectual potential or ability. Meaning-making level is a developmental measure of how individuals organize their experience, which evolves over time. Students at order 3 are not less intellectually capable than students at order 4. Learning difficulties experienced by order 3 meaning-makers in order 4 environments are not due to learning deficits; they are due to being at a different point in their meaning-making evolution than the environment demands.

Assessing Meaning-Making Order

Recall that Mike, the order 3 meaning-maker, was a graduate student and that Amanda, the order 4 meaning-maker, had recently graduated from a master's degree program. These individual case examples are representative of what Kegan (1994) found in his longitudinal research where he and his colleagues annually interviewed a sample of graduate students for four years. The research participants were interviewed and assessed using the Subject-Object Interview (Lahey and others, 1988), which is a measure of meaning-making development based on Kegan's model. The results showed that most students' meaning-making was predominantly at order 3 or in transition between orders 3 and 4 at the beginning of the four-year period and either in transition between orders 3 and 4 or predominantly at order 4 at the end of the four years. Kegan (1994) reviews the findings of several other studies measuring his developmental model, which also indicate that the story of adult development is the gradual transition from order 3 to order 4 meaning-making. These data also suggest that "at any given moment, around one-half to two-thirds of the adult population appears not to have fully reached the fourth order of consciousness" (p. 188).

Given these data, we can project that most traditional-aged undergraduate students and many non-traditional-aged undergraduates are either predominantly making meaning at order 3 or in transition from order 3 to order 4. Of course, this is not reflective of the meaning-making of any particular individual. To assess individual meaning-making, faculty must listen carefully to what students say about their understanding of their experiences, including how they make sense of learning experiences, their relationships with others, and themselves. In particular, faculty should listen to what individual students describe as needed support from faculty. This provides one avenue for assessing meaning-making order and, simultaneously, considering what a particular student expects from faculty.

I interviewed student affairs interns and professionals about what they thought they needed from their supervisors to feel supported in their work (Ignelzi, 1994). Though the relationship between supervisors and supervisees is somewhat different from those between faculty and students, there are some commonalties regarding the basic learning and teaching process evident in both types of relationships.

Stephanie, an order 3 meaning-maker, stated that she needed her supervisor to validate that she was doing things right and in a way that her supervisor liked:

> There are some times I just need to go in and just have her validate that what I'm doing is OK or I'm on the right track. It's just nice to run by what I'm doing and know that there's support there. That she, you know, that she's agreeing, that what I'm doing is good. . . . I feel comfortable knowing that there's, that she's supporting what I'm doing and that she's listening and that she seems excited about what I'm doing, that she likes my answers or my directions, what I'm coming up with [p. 130].

Sam, a transitional order 3–4 meaning-maker, appreciated that his supervisor allowed him the freedom to do things differently but still relied on his supervisor's feedback to evaluate himself:

> Aside from him being available and interested, the part that's nicest is that he'll allow you to try something different. . . . He comes from the frame of mind that, you know, if you can find a better way to do it, then do it your way. . . . I think as long as the end result is the same, he'll let you take whatever path you feel most comfortable with to get there. . . . And he gives me ongoing feedback. . . . I haven't had any surprises from him really in terms of how I've been performing. . . . That's important to me [p. 158].

Sarah, an order 4 meaning-maker, discussed how her view of her supervisor had changed to a collegial one:

> I guess I've come to see that I do the work I do; I take feedback from her, and some of the feedback she's given me has been very helpful. At the same time, I know that we're all working in this together, and she's had some more experience . . . but what I have to say is also very important and has worth. . . . I see us as very much like equals, in that we're dealing with the same situations. . . . She has some different responsibilities than I do, but it still comes back to we're all colleagues [p. 205].

As these three interview excerpts demonstrate, the way individuals view their relationship with their supervisors and what they want from their supervisors can be quite different and is influenced by meaning-making order. Translating this material to the learning and teaching context, it can be projected that these individuals would view the role of faculty differently as well. Stephanie would want a great deal of feedback and validation from her professor as she relies on external sources in helping her co-construct her views of knowledge and herself as learner. Sam wants to have some limited autonomy to try new approaches to learning as his own internal self-standards are developing, but he would still need instructor feedback to help him monitor and evaluate his performance. Sarah has reconstructed her view of the teacher-learner relationship to fit her sense of self-authorship, viewing the professor as peer and colleague in the learning endeavor.

Supporting Development Toward Self-Authorship

If, as suggested earlier, a central goal of higher education should be the achievement of self-authorship, how can faculty encourage its development while not contributing to students' experience of being "in over their heads"? In other words, how can faculty provide appropriate support and challenge that will facilitate the developmental transition from order 3 to order 4 meaning-making? Returning to the earlier "farm" metaphor may provide some guidance.

1. *Visit and appreciate the other people's farm before trying to get them to consider moving to that new farm up the road.* Supporting someone's development first requires comprehending and valuing how the other person currently understands his or her experience. Kegan (1982) suggests that to be of effective help to another, we need to be able to communicate that we understand how it is for them. This act creates the interpersonal connection that is so important to order 3 meaning-makers: to feel supported by the external sources with whom they currently co-construct their meaning.

2. *Give the students good directions on how to get to the new farm or, better still, accompany them on the trip.* Giving students tasks that require order 4 meaning-making while providing them with little structure, guidance, or support does not facilitate becoming self-authored. A professor cannot tell students how to become self-authored in their learning but can provide learning experiences that provide incrementally-structured supervised practice in moving toward generating one's own ideas and theories about course material. Critical thinking exercises, ethical dilemma discussions, and journal writing are all valuable teaching methods in this process.

3. *Encourage students to travel together to visit the new farm.* Group work is a powerful developmental tool in facilitating movement from order 3 to order 4 meaning-making. The process of the developmental transition between order 3 and 4 is one of slowly creating and distinguishing one's own view from the view that is co-constructed with others. Students placed in learning groups will likely be at different points in this developmental process. As they work on tasks together, those closer to order 4 meaning-making will assert their more self-authored views and encourage their peers to articulate and assume responsibility for their own.

4. *Provide opportunities for celebrating the move to the new farm and reminiscing about leaving the old one.* The move toward self-authorship should be reinforced and celebrated as it progresses, through appropriate feedback, evaluation, and congratulatory acknowledgments. Likewise, students should be given opportunities to reflect on their thoughts and feelings about leaving the comfort of co-constructing the self to the somewhat frightening order 4 recognition that one is in charge of and responsible for one's own experience and self-construction. The transition to self-authorship involves reconstruction not only of how the self makes meaning of knowledge but

also of how the self makes meaning of relationships with others and the self. Fears about losing one's relational and psychological connection with others are perceived as real and need to be contradicted by important others (faculty, peers, family) standing by and with the student through this developmental transition.

The collegiate environment provides more developmental challenge (and demands) than support for students navigating the transition to self-authorship. Therefore, it is important for faculty to ensure that adequate support is also provided. Kegan (1994) asserts that educators must be about building developmental bridges that are *meaningful* to the students' current meaning-making and *facilitative* of a more complex way. He states, "We cannot simply stand on our favored side of the bridge and worry or fume about the many who have not yet passed over. A bridge must be well anchored on both sides, with as much respect for where it begins as for where it ends" (p. 62).

References

Baxter Magolda, M. B. *Knowing and Reasoning in College: Gender-Related Patterns in Students' Intellectual Development.* San Francisco: Jossey-Bass, 1992.

Ignelzi, M. G. "A Description of Student Affairs Professional Development in the Supervisory Context and an Analysis of Its Relation to Constructive Development." Unpublished doctoral dissertation, Harvard University, 1994.

Johnson, J. E., and Hooper, F. E. "Piagetian Structuralism and Learning: Two Decades of Educational Application." *Contemporary Educational Psychology,* 1982, 7, 217–237.

Kegan, R. *The Evolving Self: Problem and Process in Human Development.* Cambridge, Mass.: Harvard University Press, 1982.

Kegan, R. *In over Our Heads: The Mental Demands of Modern Life.* Cambridge, Mass.: Harvard University Press, 1994.

Kegan, R., Noam, G. G., and Rogers, L. "The Psychologic of Emotion: A Neo-Piagetian View." In D. Chichetti and P. Pogge-Hesse (eds.), *Emotional Development.* San Francisco: Jossey-Bass, 1982.

King, P. M., and Baxter Magolda, M. B. "A Developmental Perspective on Learning." *Journal of College Student Development,* 1996, 37, 163–173.

King, P. M., and Kitchener, K. S. *Developing Reflective Judgment: Understanding and Promoting Intellectual Growth and Critical Thinking in Adolescents and Adults.* San Francisco: Jossey-Bass, 1994.

Kohlberg, L. *The Psychology of Moral Development.* San Francisco: HarperSanFrancisco, 1984.

Lahey, L., and others. "A Guide to the Subject-Object Interview: Its Administration and Interpretation." Unpublished manuscript, Harvard University, 1988.

Perry, W. G., Jr. *Forms of Intellectual and Ethical Development in the College Years: A Scheme.* Austin, Tex.: Holt, Rinehart and Winston, 1970.

Piaget, J. *Six Psychological Studies.* New York: Vintage, 1967.

MICHAEL IGNELZI *is assistant professor of counseling and educational psychology and graduate program coordinator for student personnel at Slippery Rock University in Slippery Rock, Pennsylvania.*

2

*Helping students make sound judgments is a common
teaching goal for faculty members. This chapter explains
how students' approaches to making judgments are
grounded in their assumptions about knowledge and
how it is gained.*

Learning to Make Reflective Judgments

Patricia M. King

Professors take great pride in encouraging students to think in more informed, subtle, and sophisticated ways. Cultivating good thinking is one of the most rewarding and important outcomes of teaching, for good thinking is a truly generalizable skill that students can use in many contexts beyond the confines of one course, one field of study, or one major decision. This is also a challenging undertaking. For example, consider the following exchange, which was overheard between a professor and a student in a history class.

PROFESSOR: Class, today we continue our discussion of the Renaissance. This was such a remarkable era! It's sustained my scholarly interest for my whole career, and I hope you will find it equally stimulating and rewarding to study. Before we begin, are there any questions from our last class?

STUDENT: Yes, I think I followed everything from last time, but I just can't seem to find in my notes when the Renaissance started.

PROFESSOR: Oh, that is a very good question! You see, the Renaissance in northern Italy really took hold at a different time and in a different context than the Renaissance in the south. This is important because—

STUDENT *(interrupting)*: Sir, I was hoping you could answer my question *before* you got started today.

PROFESSOR: Yes. In determining when the Renaissance got started, it's also important to recognize that this "awakening" covered many aspects of people's lives. Why, the scientific Renaissance and the ideas of Leonardo da Vinci had such tremendous potential, made ever richer by the emergence of the artistic Renaissance and artists such as Michelangelo and

STUDENT *(interrupting and now irritated)*: Sir! *Before* you start today's lecture, could you please just state when the Renaissance began?

NEW DIRECTIONS FOR TEACHING AND LEARNING, no. 82, Summer 2000   © Jossey-Bass Publishers

PROFESSOR: April 14, 1363.
STUDENT: Thank you, sir. That's all I wanted to know.

Such exchanges show the frustrations and misunderstandings that can emerge when there is a wide discrepancy between students' and professors' expectations about courses and what should happen there. Both hold many expectations about teaching and learning, reflecting their prior experiences and their personal philosophies. These expectations reflect what they think is important to learn, how it should be learned, who has what responsibilities in the teacher-student relationship, how much time and energy should be devoted to the course, and so on.

One important element that underlies expectations about the teaching and learning process is the assumptions a person holds about knowledge and how it is gained; these are termed *epistemological assumptions* because they are based on the area of philosophy called epistemology, the study of the nature and origin of knowledge. (For a recent compilation of theory and research on epistemological theories, see Hofer and Pintrich, in press.) Many students report that they "learned how to think" in college; cognitive psychologists and higher education researchers (Pascarella and Terenzini, 1991; Hofer and Pintrich, 1997; Tsui, 1999) have conducted studies confirming that many students do show gains in critical thinking during college. The remainder of this chapter will focus on one line of research that has documented development in reasoning during the college years based on changes in epistemological assumptions, research on the Reflective Judgment Model (King and Kitchener, 1994, in press). This model of late adolescent and adult intellectual development is grounded in John Dewey's work (1933, 1938) on reflective thinking. Reflective thinking is necessary when a person wants to come to a judgment (a "reflective judgment") about a problematic or vexing issue that cannot be answered by formal logic alone. This model shows how people's epistemological assumptions are related to the ways they reason about controversial issues.

The Reflective Judgment Model

Many professors endorse two interrelated goals for students: (1) to evaluate knowledge claims more fully and (2) to explain and defend their points of view on controversial issues more convincingly. The Reflective Judgment Model can be used to help faculty understand the steps that students often take to achieve these goals. This model describes a developmental progression that occurs between childhood and adulthood in the ways that people understand the process of knowing and the certainty of knowledge claims and in the corresponding ways that they justify their beliefs.

The following verbatim comments were made in a discussion of the controversy surrounding the safety of food additives. (Examples are from Lynch, Kitchener, and King, 1994, pp. 83–85; "I" stands for interviewer and

"R" for respondent.) Each comment reflects one of the three major categories of thinking styles in this model: prereflective, quasi-reflective, and reflective thinking.

Example of Prereflective Thinking
Certainty of Knowledge

I: Can you ever know for sure that your position that NutraSweet is safe is correct?

R: No, I don't know for sure because I don't manufacture it.

I: OK. Do you think we'll ever know for sure?

R: If somebody more or less has the guts to stand up and go and do all the research on it and find out.

I: Do you think someday we'll know?

R: Yes.

Justification of Beliefs

I: When people differ about the safety of NutraSweet and matters like this, is it the case that one opinion is right and the other is wrong?

R: Some people's opinions are right, and they can more or less prove that they are right, and the other people that think they're wrong maybe can't prove it.

I: So you think that some people indeed are right?

R: Yes.

I: And "right" in what way? What do you mean by "right"?

R: They can back their opinions, have the facts to show that they are right.

Students who hold epistemological assumptions associated with prereflective thinking believe that knowledge is gained through the word of an authority figure (such as a scientist, a priest, or a professor) or through firsthand observation. The use of evidence is not a salient characteristic of reasoning at this level. These individuals believe that what they know is absolutely correct and that they know it with complete certainty. They do not often acknowledge the problematic aspects of what for others is a vexing issue.

Example of Quasi-Reflective Thinking
Certainty of Knowledge

I: Can you ever say you know for sure that chemicals are safe?

R: No, I don't think so.

I: Can you tell me why you'll never know for sure?

R: Because they test them on little animals, and they haven't really tested them in humans, as far as I know. And I don't think anything is for sure.

I: When people differ about matters such as this, is it the case that one opinion is right and one is wrong?

R: No. I think it just depends on how you feel personally.

Justification of Beliefs

I: When people differ about matters such as this, is it the case that one opinion is right and one opinion is wrong?

R: Not necessarily, because people make their decisions based upon how they feel and what research they've seen. So what one person thinks is right, another person might think is wrong; but that doesn't make it wrong. It has to be a personal decision. If I feel that chemicals cause cancer and you feel that food is unsafe without [them], your opinion might be right to you and my opinion is right to me.

I: Could we ever say that one opinion is better and one is worse?

R: I don't think so.

I: Can you tell me why not?

R: Just because the opinion that a person has is based upon what he believes, and so you wouldn't be able to say that one person's opinion is better than another's because it's just an opinion.

Students who reason using quasi-reflective assumptions recognize that knowledge claims contain elements of uncertainty due to missing information or to differences or errors in data-gathering methods. They use evidence in decision making, but inconsistently, and often appear confused about how evidence thus seen as uncertain can be used to reach a conclusion. They tend to view judgments as highly idiosyncratic and to be very skeptical of attempts to evaluate judgments and other "opinions." This skepticism may be seen as they try to understand faculty grading of essays or other "subjective" papers.

Example of Reflective Thinking

Certainty of Knowledge

I: How is it that experts, two chemists, for example, might disagree about this issue?

R: Because our research sciences are not exact, because there are differences in controls used, differences in intensities of materials, and so on, as well as differences in interpretation.

I: And I also heard you say [earlier] that you would take this point of view as being the best you could do right now.

R: Right. I still can't accept that I could be absolutely one hundred percent positive, especially if I just looked in one journal, or two journals, or even five or ten. If I were a chemist and conducted the experiments, I might know even more than I could know now. This is what I'm finding out. The more education I get, the more uncertain I am about things. . . . But when it comes down to a point of food additives, or specific food additives, you do need to operate on what you think is best at the time, the best information you can get, and act accordingly.

Justification of Beliefs

I: How would you define the "better" option?

R: One that takes as many factors as possible into consideration. I mean one that uses the [highest] percentage of the data that we have, and perhaps that uses the methodology that has been most reliable.

I: And how did you come to your conclusions as to what the evidence suggests?

R: I think you have to take a look at the different opinions and studies that are offered by different groups. Maybe some studies offered by the chemical industry, some studies by the government, and some private studies— a variety of studies from a variety of different areas. You wouldn't trust, for instance, a study funded by the tobacco industry that proved cigarette smoking is not harmful. You wouldn't base your point of view entirely upon that study. Things like that have to be taken into account also. Because unfortunately, when you get into the area of money, making money and making a profit, not only do you have to interpret the scientific evidence, but you have to try to interpret people's motives also, and that makes it an even more complex soup to try to strain out.

People who reason using reflective thinking assumptions accept uncertainty in decision making but are not immobilized by it. They are willing to endorse conclusions as "most reasonable" and about which they are "reasonably certain." These conclusions are explicitly based on their evaluation of the available data. They believe that knowledge claims must be evaluated in relation to the context in which they were generated to determine their validity; that any claim should be reevaluated in light of new data, new methodologies, and new perspectives on the question; and that they must actively construct their own decisions.

Each of these three pairs of examples illustrates how the way a student reasons about a controversial or vexing problem is related to his or her epistemological assumptions. Each successive level is more complex, reflecting both sophistication and appreciation for subtlety in reasoning skills. More specifically, the relationship between evidence and judgment becomes more explicit and more salient across levels.

These brief descriptions of the three major categories of reflective thinking are drawn from a much more detailed seven-stage model of Reflective Judgment. For a full description of the stages (and for a description of the "complex stage" model that defines their use of the term "stage," see King and Kitchener's compendium of Reflective Judgment theory, research, and practice (1994). All seven stages of the Reflective Judgment Model are summarized in Exhibit 2.1.

Exhibit 2.1. Summary: The Seven Stages of Reflective Judgment

Prereflective Thinking (Stages 1, 2, and 3)

Stage 1

View of knowledge: Knowledge is assumed to exist absolutely and concretely; it is not understood as an abstraction. It can be obtained with certainty by direct observation.

Concept of justification: Beliefs need no justification since there is assumed to be an absolute correspondence between what is believed to be true and what is true. Alternate beliefs are not perceived.

"I know what I have seen."

Stage 2

View of knowledge: Knowledge is assumed to be absolutely certain or certain but not immediately available. Knowledge can be obtained directly through the senses (as in direct observation) or via authority figures.

Concept of justification: Beliefs are unexamined and unjustified or justified by their correspondence with the beliefs of an authority figure (such as a teacher or parent). Most issues are assumed to have a right answer, so there is little or no conflict in making decisions about disputed issues.

"If it is on the news, it has to be true."

Stage 3

View of knowledge: Knowledge is assumed to be absolutely certain or temporarily uncertain. In areas of temporary uncertainty, only personal beliefs can be known until absolute knowledge is obtained. In areas of absolute certainty, knowledge is obtained from authorities.

Concept of justification: In areas in which certain answers exist, beliefs are justified by reference to authorities' views. In areas in which answers do not exist, beliefs are defended as personal opinion since the link between evidence and beliefs is unclear.

*"When there is evidence that people can give to convince everybody
one way or another, then it will be knowledge; until then, it's just a guess."*

Quasi-Reflective Thinking (Stages 4 and 5)

Stage 4

View of knowledge: Knowledge is uncertain and knowledge claims are idiosyncratic to the individual since situational variables (such as incorrect reporting of data, data lost over time, or disparities in access to information) dictate that knowing always involves an element of ambiguity.

Concept of justification: Beliefs are justified by giving reasons and using evidence, but the arguments and choice of evidence are idiosyncratic (for example, choosing evidence that fits an established belief).

*"I'd be more inclined to believe evolution if they had proof. It's just like the pyramids:
I don't think we'll ever know. Who are you going to ask? No one was there."*

Stage 5

View of knowledge: Knowledge is contextual and subjective since it is filtered through a person's perceptions and criteria for judgment. Only interpretations of evidence, events, or issues may be known.

Concept of justification: Beliefs are justified within a particular context by means of the rules of inquiry for that context and by context-specific interpretations of evidence. Specific beliefs are assumed to be context specific or are balanced against other interpretations, which complicates (and sometimes delays) conclusions.

*"People think differently and so they attack the problem differently.
Other theories could be as true as my own, but based on different evidence."*

Reflective Thinking (Stages 6 and 7)

Stage 6

View of knowledge: Knowledge is constructed into individual conclusions about ill-structured problems on the basis of information from a variety of sources. Interpretations that are based on evaluations of evidence across contexts and on the evaluated opinions of reputable others can be known.

Concept of justification: Beliefs are justified by comparing evidence and opinion from different perspectives on an issue or across different contexts and by constructing solutions that are evaluated by criteria such as the weight of the evidence, the utility of the solution, or the pragmatic need for action.

"It's very difficult in this life to be sure. There are degrees of sureness.
You come to a point at which you are sure enough for a personal stance on the issue."

Stage 7

View of knowledge: Knowledge is the outcome of a process of reasonable inquiry in which solutions to ill-structured problems are constructed. The adequacy of those solutions is evaluated in terms of what is most reasonable or probable according to the current evidence, and it is reevaluated when relevant new evidence, perspectives, or tools of inquiry become available.

Concept of justification: Beliefs are justified probabilistically on the basis of a variety of interpretive considerations, such as the weight of the evidence, the explanatory value of the interpretations, the risk of erroneous conclusions, consequences of alternative judgments, and the interrelationships of these factors. Conclusions are defended as representing the most complete, plausible or compelling understanding of an issue on the basis of the available evidence.

"One can judge an argument by how well thought-out the positions are,
what kinds of reasoning and evidence are used to support it, and how consistent
the way one argues on this topic is as compared with other topics."

Source: King, P. M., and Kitchener, K. S. (1994). *Developing Reflective Judgment.* pp. 14–16. Reprinted by permission of Jossey-Bass, Inc., a division of John Wiley & Sons, Inc.

Research on the Development of Reflective Judgment

The verbatim examples given earlier represent a range of reflective judgment levels. Which are the most common sets of assumptions among college students? Do they vary by educational level? How does reflective judgment relate to other aspects of development? Fortunately, the Reflective Judgment Model has an extensive research base gathered over the past twenty years to inform these questions.

King and Kitchener (1994) reported the results of dozens of studies on the development of reflective judgment. Wood (1997) conducted a comprehensive secondary analysis of data from more than two thousand individuals in all previously reported studies. Longitudinal studies have consistently shown upward changes in reflective judgment over time, especially among individuals involved in educational endeavors. Further, these changes generally followed the posited sequence of stages, with higher-stage usage following lower-stage usage.

Educational level is strongly associated with reflective thinking: a clear, developmental progression may be observed in the reflective judgment scores from high school to college, from the first year to the senior year of college, from college to graduate school, and from early (master's degree) to advanced (third-year doctoral) graduate programs. Since teaching reasoning skills such as the development, analysis, and critique of knowledge claims is a commonly cited educational goal for many colleges and universities, many educators find this clear progression reassuring evidence of their success. Indeed, the finding of significant differences between the scores of the freshmen and seniors suggests that important shifts in epistemological assumptions are occurring during the college years. Specifically, the senior scores reflect an acceptance of uncertainty as a natural part of the knowing process; they also reflect movement from beliefs based on "what feels right" or "what I want to believe" to beliefs based (at least partly) on evidence. Kroll (1992) termed this type of developmental progression the abandonment of "ignorant certainty" in favor of "intelligent confusion." Many seniors also show deeper understanding of different points of view, such as how one's perspective affects the kinds of data one gathers and which data one weighs more heavily.

However, this assessment of educational progress tells only part of the story. The reflective judgment scores of most college students show that their reasoning reflects the assumptions of quasi-reflective thinking, not reflective thinking. Among the student samples, only the advanced doctoral students have consistently reasoned reflectively. While "intelligent confusion" appears to be an important step toward reflective thinking, it not the aim of undergraduate education.

Reflective judgment also appears to be related to other dimensions of development, including moral reasoning and reasoning about diversity issues (King and Shuford, 1996). Several studies (summarized in King and Kitchener, 1994) have found a moderate positive relationship between the kinds of assumptions students use to reason about intellectual issues (their epistemological assumptions) and the assumptions they use to reason about moral issues (their assumptions about what is right, fair, and good). Guthrie, King, and Palmer (1999) found moderate positive correlations between reflective thinking and tolerance for diversity. More strikingly, the reflective judgment scores accounted for almost half of the variance in tolerance scores: participants in this study who reasoned at quasi-reflective and reflective thinking levels were much more likely to hold tolerant viewpoints with respect to race and sexual orientation than their counterparts who held prereflective assumptions.

King and Howard-Hamilton (1999) found that the development of multicultural competence also appears to parallel development in reflective thinking. They asked a sample of diversity education experts to describe early, middle, and advanced levels of multicultural competence. The experts' descriptions of these levels mirrored the assumptions of prereflective, quasi-reflective, and reflective thinking, respectively. It may be that there is a cognitive component underlying the development of multicultural competence—for example, that being able to think reflectively is a precursor to being able to apply those skills to one's addressing and understanding multicultural issues. If so, this would be further evidence of interdependence among supposedly distinct aspects of development.

Findings like these about relationships across areas of development are important for educators to understand because they remind us that development evolves holistically, that assisting college students to achieve their educational goals involves several interrelated elements, not just reasoning skills. Unfortunately, these elements are often addressed discretely. For example, faculty members often see their teaching role as challenging and sharpening the intellect. Concomitantly, they often presume that the responsibility for challenging and fostering other aspects of development (such as character or sense of identity) lies with others, such as parents or student affairs staff. I refer to this peculiar distribution of educational responsibilities as the "cut them off at the neck" approach, which is ill-founded for a variety of reasons. For example, there is plentiful evidence not only that major aspects of development are interrelated but also that poorly developed skills in one area of development can inhibit competence in other areas (Kegan, 1994; King and Baxter Magolda, 1996; Kitchener, 1982). Many faculty have witnessed good students performing poorly on oral reports because they lack the confidence to speak in front of their peers or submitting "wishy-washy" opinion or editorial essays because they do not consider themselves smart enough to offer their own opinions. A student who appreciates why people approach controversial issues in her discipline from different perspectives is more likely to see and appreciate the reasons people approach social controversies from different perspectives. By the same token, a student who evaluates knowledge claims in his major by reference to the strength of the evidence in support of conflicting hypotheses would also be more inclined to evaluate contradictory claims about current moral issues by reference to the weight of the available evidence.

Many good teachers have long been aware of the developmental evolution of complex reasoning, and of the interrelationships among cognitive, moral, and identity development. These research findings provide strong evidence for their observations.

Creating Contexts That Help Students Think Reflectively

"In the final analysis, the challenge of college, for students and faculty members alike, is empowering individuals to know that the world is far more complex than it first appears, and that they must make interpretive arguments and decisions—judgments that entail real consequences for which they must take responsibility and from which they may not flee by disclaiming expertise" (Association of American Colleges, 1991, pp. 16–17).

How can faculty help students learn to make good interpretive arguments and decisions? Three major factors discussed here appear to be at the heart of this undertaking: understanding the knowing process in more complex and encompassing ways, accepting uncertainty without being immobilized by it, and learning to use evidence to reason to conclusions and make "best judgments." Teachers whose goals are to help students become more effective at constructing their own beliefs and knowledge claims about the world in which they live and more comfortable with their roles and responsibilities in doing so must abandon the "I pitch, you catch" view of knowledge acquisition. This approach—however commonly practiced—fails to take into account students' epistemological assumptions, their role in interpreting information, and the uncertainty in judgment making, and it is therefore ineffective in teaching students how to make reflective judgments.

Several authors have offered suggestions for promoting reflective thinking that address these factors (Davison, King, and Kitchener, 1990; King, 1992; King and Baxter Magolda, 1996; Kitchener and King, 1990; King and Wood, 1999; Kitchener, King, Wood, and Lynch, 1994; Kitchener, Lynch, Fischer, and Wood, 1993; Kroll, 1992; Kronholm, 1996; Lynch, Kitchener, and King, 1994; Wolcott and Lynch, 1997; Wood and Lynch, 1998). King and Kitchener (in press, p. 25) identified the following common suggestions from these works:

1. Show respect for students' assumptions, regardless of the developmental stage(s) they exhibit. Their assumptions are genuine and sincere reflections of their ways of making meaning, and are steps in a developmental progression. If students perceive disrespect or lack of emotional support, they may be less willing to engage in challenging discussions or to take the intellectual and personal risks required for development.

2. Discuss controversial, ill-structured issues with students throughout their educational activities, and make available resources that show the factual basis and lines of reasoning for several perspectives.

3. Create many opportunities for students to analyze *others'* points of view for evidentiary adequacy and to develop and defend their *own* points of view about controversial issues.

4. Teach students strategies for systematically gathering data, assessing the relevance of the data, evaluating data sources, and making interpretive judgments based on the available data.

5. Give students frequent feedback, and provide both cognitive and emotional support for their efforts.

6. Help students explicitly address issues of uncertainty in judgment making and examine their assumptions about knowledge and how it is gained.

7. Encourage students to practice their reasoning skills in many settings, from their other classes to their practicum sites, student organizations, residence hall councils, and elsewhere, to gain practice and confidence applying their thinking skills (p. 25).

These suggestions presume that teachers endorse reflective thinking as an educational goal and that they apply these skills to their own decision making. However, consider the following comment made during a radio interview by a Kansas teacher in support of the 1999 Kansas State Board of Education's decision not to require the teaching of evolution in the science curriculum: "As teachers, we have an obligation to teach students the facts. Evolution is a theory, and that's a fact." Apparently, students are not the only ones who appear to be confused about the relationship between facts, theories, and interpretations.

The suggestions for promoting reflective thinking are grounded in the assumption that teachers are effective when they are good guides (Kegan, 1994; Palmer, 1998) for students' epistemological and personal learning journeys. Kroll (1992) modeled this guiding role in the ways he encouraged students to think more reflectively: "When their responses are dogmatic, I foster all their doubts; when they seem mired in skepticism or paralyzed by complexity, I push them to make judgments; when their tactics are not fully reflective, I encourage their best efforts to use critical, evaluative thinking" (p. 13). This practice shows an underlying respect for students regardless of their level of intellectual development; it acknowledges that the journey is each *student's* journey and that the teacher's role as guide is to choose responses that are adapted to the student's needs. Through respectful but challenging interactions like these, interactions that take account of students' epistemological assumptions, teachers can promote reflective thinking.

References

Association of American Colleges. *The Challenge of Connecting Learning.* Washington, D.C.: Association of American Colleges, 1991.

Davison, M. L., King, P. M., and Kitchener, K. S. "Developing Reflective Thinking and Writing." In R. Beach and S. Hynds (eds.), *Developing Discourse Practices in Adolescence and Adulthood.* Norwood, N.J.: Ablex, 1990.

Dewey, J. *How We Think: A Restatement of the Relation of Reflective Thinking to the Educative Process.* Lexington, Mass.: Heath, 1933.

Dewey, J. *Logic: The Theory of Inquiry.* Austin, Tex.: Holt, Rinehart and Winston, 1938.

Guthrie, V. L., King, P. M., and Palmer, C. P. "Cognitive Capabilities Underlying Tolerance for Diversity Among College Students." Unpublished manuscript, 1999.

Hofer, B. K., and Pintrich, P. R. "The Development of Epistemological Theories: Beliefs About Knowledge and Knowing and Their Relation to Learning." *Review of Educational Research,* 1997, 67, 88–140.

Hofer, B. K., and Pintrich, P. R. (eds.). *Personal Epistemology: The Psychology of Beliefs About Knowledge and Knowing.* Mahwah, N.J.: Erlbaum, in press.

Kegan, R. *In over Our Heads: The Mental Demands of Modern Life.* Cambridge, Mass.: Harvard University Press, 1994.

King, P. M. (ed.). "Reflective Judgment." *Journal of Liberal Education,* 1992, 78 (entire issue 1).

King, P. M., and Baxter Magolda, M. B. "A Developmental Perspective on Learning." *Journal of College Student Development,* 1996, 37, 163–173.

King, P. M., and Howard-Hamilton, M. F. "Becoming a Multiculturally Competent Student Affairs Professional." Final report submitted to the National Association of Student Personnel Association, 1999. Available from Patricia King, School of Leadership and Policy Studies, Bowling Green State University, Bowling Green, OH 43403. [http://www.naspa.org]

King, P. M., and Kitchener, K. S. *Developing Reflective Judgment: Understanding and Promoting Intellectual Growth and Critical Thinking in Adolescents and Adults.* San Francisco: Jossey-Bass, 1994.

King, P. M., and Kitchener, K. S. "The Reflective Judgment Model: Twenty Years of Research on Epistemic Cognition." In B. K. Hofer and P. R. Pintrich (eds.), *Personal Epistemology: The Psychology of Beliefs About Knowledge and Knowing.* Mahwah, N.J.: Erlbaum, in press.

King, P. M., and Shuford, B. C. "A Multicultural View Is a More Cognitively Complex View: Cognitive Development and Multicultural Education." *American Behavioral Scientist,* 1996, *40,* 153–164.

King, P. M., and Wood, P. K. "Teaching for Reflective Thinking: Why Students May Not Be Learning What We Try to Teach." Unpublished manuscript, 1999.

Kitchener, K. S. "Human Development and the College Campus: Sequences and Tasks." In G. R. Hanson (ed.), *Measuring Student Development.* New Directions for Student Services, no. 20. San Francisco: Jossey-Bass, 1982.

Kitchener, K. S., and King, P. M. "The Reflective Judgment Model: Transforming Assumptions About Knowing." In J. Mesirow and Associates, *Fostering Critical Reflection in Adulthood: A Guide to Transformative and Emancipatory Learning.* San Francisco: Jossey-Bass, 1990.

Kitchener, K. S., King, P. M., Wood, P. K, and Lynch, C. L. "Assessing Reflective Thinking in Curricular Contexts." Technical report of the Reflective Thinking Appraisal, Fund for the Improvement of Postsecondary Education, Application No. P116B00926, 1994.

Kitchener, K. S., Lynch, C. L., Fischer, K. W., and Wood, P. K. "Developmental Range of Reflective Judgment: The Effect of Contextual Support and Practice on Developmental Stage." *Developmental Psychology,* 1993, *29* (5), 893–906.

Kroll, B. M. *Teaching Hearts and Minds: College Students Reflect on the Vietnam War in Literature.* Carbondale: Southern Illinois University Press, 1992.

Kronholm, M. M. "The Impact of Developmental Instruction on Reflective Judgment." *Review of Higher Education,* 1993, *19,* 199–225.

Lynch, C. L., Kitchener, K. S., and King, P. M. "Developing Reflective Judgment in the Classroom: A Manual for Faculty." Report of Foundation for the Improvement of Postsecondary Education Project No. P116B00926, 1994. Available from Cindy Lynch, HCR 75, P.O. Box 91, New Concord, KY 42076.

Palmer, P. J. *The Courage to Teach: Exploring the Inner Landscape of a Teacher's Life.* San Francisco: Jossey-Bass, 1998.

Pascarella, E. T., and Terenzini, P. T. *How College Affects Students: Findings and Insights from Twenty Years of Research.* San Francisco: Jossey-Bass, 1991.

Tsui, L. "Courses and Instruction Affecting Critical Thinking." *Research in Higher Education,* 1999, *40,* 185–200.

Wolcott, S. K., and Lynch, C. L. "Critical Thinking in the Accounting Classroom: A Reflective Judgment Developmental Process Perspective." *Accounting Education,* 1997, *2,* 59–78.

Wood, P. K. "A Secondary Analysis of Claims Regarding the Reflective Judgment Interview: Internal Consistency, Sequentiality, and Inter-Individual Differences in Ill-Structured Problem Solving." In J. C. Smart (ed.), *Higher Education: Handbook of Theory and Research,* Vol. 12. Edison, N.J.: Agathon Press, 1997.

Wood, P. K., and Lynch, C. L. "Using Guided Essays to Assess and Encourage Reflective Thinking." *Assessment Update,* 1998, *10* (2), 14–15.

PATRICIA M. KING *is professor and director, School of Leadership and Policy Studies, at Bowling Green State University in Bowling Green, Ohio.*

3

A "connected education" would cultivate connections among students, between students and teachers, and between students and their work. Stories of ways of knowing show how pedagogy can create contexts for these connections.

Toward a More Connected Vision of Higher Education

Blythe McVicker Clinchy

A few years ago, I visited a class at my college in which the teacher, a philosopher, was trying to guide a group of first-year students through a discussion of the arguments made in Darwin's time for and against the universe having been created by God. When the discussion showed signs of deteriorating into an exchange of personal beliefs, the teacher admonished the students: "Remember, we're not talking about beliefs here. We're talking about *arguments* for beliefs." I thought to myself, what a wonderful thing for these first-year students to hear. What an important distinction that is—between the reasonableness of an argument and the belief the argument is supporting. I felt proud to be a member of an institution that understood and exemplified the value of detachment, the capacity to stand aside from one's beliefs and look at them objectively.

I continue to honor the capacity for detachment, and I still try to cultivate it in my students. But I have learned that for many women students, even some of the most successful ones, detachment can lead to indifference, even alienation. Rightly or wrongly, they believe that the system demands that they remove themselves from their work. Simone, for instance, says that she can write "good papers," papers teachers like, and "someday," she hopes, she might be able to write papers that she likes, but at the moment, she doesn't like them: "I do it, and I get my grade," she says, "but it hasn't proved anything to me. The problem is that I don't feel terribly strongly about one point of view, but that point of view seems to make more sense. It's easier to write the paper, supporting that point of view than the other one, because there's more to support it. And it's not one of my deep-founded beliefs, but it writes the paper." Simone has learned to distinguish between beliefs and arguments for beliefs. Her papers contain no beliefs, only arguments. In fact, Simone does not write the paper; "it" writes the paper. Reasons write the paper, and reasons seem unrelated to personal truth.

Stories like Simone's have convinced me that the values, goals, structure, and pedagogical practices of our institutions of higher education are imbalanced. Something goes wrong, at least for women, when we subject them to an education that emphasizes separation and detachment to the virtual exclusion of connection and attachment.

My thoughts on these matters have been formed largely by interviews conducted mainly, though not exclusively, with women, over a number of years. I will draw principally on two studies: first, a longitudinal study done at my own institution, Wellesley College, a liberal arts college for women, with my colleague Claire Zimmerman, in which we interviewed several cohorts of undergraduates annually throughout their four years at the college (Clinchy and Zimmerman, 1982; 1985), and second, a project carried out with three other developmental psychologists, Mary Belenky, Nancy Goldberger, and Jill Tarule, involving interviews with 135 women of varying ages and social and ethnic backgrounds, among them undergraduates and alumnae from a range of educational institutions, including relatively "progressive" colleges and an inner-city community college, as well as Wellesley. This research formed the basis for our book, *Women's Ways of Knowing (WWK)* (Belenky, Clinchy, Goldberger, and Tarule, [1986] 1997). In both studies, we tried to elicit our informants' conceptions of knowledge and truth, and we invited them to give us accounts of their educational experiences. In this chapter, I refer mainly to women, because both of these studies and nearly all of my teaching has focused on women, but I believe that colleges do a disservice to men as well. Although gender is beyond the focus of this article, a discussion of the relation of gender and ways of knowing can be found in Clinchy and Norem, 1998.

Epistemological Positions

In *WWK*, we described five different perspectives on knowledge that the women we interviewed seemed to hold. Like William Perry (1970), we call these perspectives "positions." The perspectives we've identified are similar to his, although different in some important respects. Most of them will be familiar to anyone who works with college students.

Received Knowing. For the received knower, Truth (spelled with a capital *T*) is absolute and straightforward, and it lies in the hands of (capital *A*) Authorities. To illustrate: in one of our studies, we said to our interviewees, "Suppose two people disagree on the interpretation of a poem. How would you decide which one is right?" A sophomore replied, "You'd have to ask the poet. It's his poem." We came to call this perspective "received knowledge" because the knower at this position acts essentially as a receptacle. She cannot create ideas or evaluate them. If Authority fails to dispense the Truth, she is at a loss. As one student said, "I like it when teachers do the talking, because notes are easy to take. . . . When students talk, you don't know whether it's right or not, and then you don't know whether to write it down."

Subjective Knowing. Subjectivism is in some respects the opposite of received knowledge. For the received knower, truth is utterly objective: "Science," a received knower told us, "is not a creation of the human mind." For subjectivists, truth resides in the heart or the gut: "Whatever feels right is right for me." Responding to our question about the interpretation of a poem, one student said, "I find that when ideas are being tossed around, I'm usually more akin to one than another. I don't know—my opinions are just sort of there." And another said, "Well, with me it's almost more a matter of liking one more than another. I mean, I happen to agree with one or identify with it more." For the subjectivist, truth is almost entirely a creation of the human mind, almost utterly subjective: "Whatever you see in the poem, it's got to be there." Here the external world seems almost to disappear. The words on the page dissolve into a sort of Rorschach inkblot, exerting little constraint on the meaning the reader projects onto the page.

Domain Specificity and Epistemological Preference. This does not mean that students operate out of the same epistemological perspective in all areas of their lives; often they view different parts of the curriculum from different perspectives. For instance, naive undergraduates typically perceive the humanities as largely subjective and mathematics and science as largely objective. A sophomore expressed this worldview: "In science, you can be more objective because someone's already said, you know, 'if you see something that looks like this, well then, it's' whatever it is. . . . You know, if a bacteria looks a certain shape, it's called this. Then they're objective, and you can't do anything about the shape of them." With literature and history, she said, it's different: "You can just twist [them] around to suit yourself."

Epistemological positions operate as learning preferences or styles that guide a student's choice of academic concentration. In a survey distributed as part of the Pathways Project (Rayman and Brett, 1993) at Wellesley, students were asked to respond to the statement "I prefer subject matter with precise answers to subject matter with multiple interpretations." This question discriminated significantly, and more than any other, between students who said upon entering the college that they planned to major in math or science and those who said they planned to major in social sciences or humanities. It discriminated, more than any other question, between students who at the end of the sophomore year stuck with their plan to major in math or science and those who switched to a nonscience major. Here is a student who opts for a major in the humanities: "I don't like science courses because things are just too concrete. I like it when the teacher accepts your opinion as being as valid as his or hers and doesn't try to dictate to you what is the right, correct way to interpret something or to look at something, because there just is not one way to look at things. And one's entitled to think for [oneself]." And here is one who chooses science: "I take mostly science courses, quantitative courses, 'cause there there's mostly one truth, one right answer. I don't like qualitative courses like philosophy, 'cause they're so ambiguous. Everything's all relative, it's just opinion, and I don't see much use for it."

When I share these comments with colleagues, they are dismayed. Science teachers protest that science is not just a matter of counting and naming things, that it does involve interpretation, and that although science may be more objective than philosophy—there is, after, all, a real world out there—nonetheless, it is a creation of the human mind. And teachers in the humanities protest that although students are of course entitled to think for themselves, they are obligated to *think,* to construct reasonable interpretations, grounded in the text.

Like most of the teachers I respect, I want my students to pay close attention to whatever it is we're studying. I don't want them just to swallow my interpretations of a text or wallow in their own gut reactions to it. I want them to examine ideas closely, whether the ideas originate in a text, a classmate's comment, a teacher's lecture, or their own minds. Students who rely exclusively on the relatively passive modes of Received or subjective knowledge are not really thinking. The received knower's ideas come ready-made from the professor; the subjectivist's opinions are "just there." Neither the received knower nor the subjectivist has any systematic, deliberate procedures for developing new ideas or for testing the validity of ideas. What college seems to do for many students is help them develop such procedures.

Procedural Knowing. Students who have reached the position of procedural knowing no longer believe that they can acquire knowledge or arrive at truth through immediate apprehension. Knowledge does not consist of facts to be stored "as is" or of the static residue of direct experience. Knowledge is a *process,* and it requires work. Although no single "answer" may be "right," all interpretations are not equally valid. Knowing requires the application of procedures for comparing and contrasting and constructing interpretations, and the quality of the knowledge depends on the skill of the knower. In *WWK,* we identified two broad types of procedures, labeling them "separate" and "connected" knowing.

Separate Knowing. Separate knowing involves critical thinking. It is "critical" in the sense of "discerning," as in the Greek *kritikos*; it also has an adversarial flavor. For example, when I ask my students to consider what other interpretations a scientist might have made of the experimental results the scientist has reported, I am asking them to engage in separate knowing. For an undergraduate we call Jane, separate knowing had become almost a reflex: She said, "As soon as someone tells me his point of view, I immediately start arguing in my head the opposite point of view. When someone is saying something, I can't help turning it upside down." Like many of the students we interviewed, Jane has learned to argue with the person she is reading or listening to. Whether she argues in her head, on paper, or out loud, she looks for flaws in the object, generating opposing ideas, perhaps conjuring up contradictory evidence. She plays what the writer-teacher Peter Elbow calls the "doubting game" (1973; 1986). The doubting game is very popular in the halls of academe: we use it in our teaching, and we try to teach our students to use it. Some of us seem, like Jane, to have developed an adversarial reflex that operates almost as a compulsion. The literary critic David Bleich, for instance, calls attention to "the habit of adversarial reasoning in scholarly work." In the academy, he says, it is assumed that ideas must "compete" with one another: for example, "To justify new work on a topic, graduate students are trained—some would say 'forced'—to review the literature and say why it is inadequate; new work can only be done if others have 'failed to note' it" (1990, pp. 241–242).

Nancy, another undergraduate, provides an especially clear illustration of this aspect of separate knowing: "I never take anything someone says for granted. I just tend to see the contrary. I like playing devil's advocate, arguing the opposite of what somebody's saying, thinking of exceptions to what the person has said or thinking of a different train of logic." Nancy takes an impersonal stance toward the argument she is examining. The person she is reading or talking with could be anyone. She herself could be anyone. There is no personal relationship between the two. Only the product matters; the person who produced it is irrelevant. We academicians tend to place a high value on impersonality. For example, some of us pride ourselves on "blind grading": we read and evaluate students' papers without knowing who wrote them so as not to let our feelings about the person affect our evaluation of the product. And we try to teach our students to examine the material we are studying with a detached, objective eye. This is indeed a powerful way of knowing, but the students we interviewed taught us that there is another equally powerful way.

Connected Knowing. In the Wellesley study, we asked students to respond to comments like Jane's and Nancy's, illustrating critical thinking, and although some of them agreed with the two women, many did not. Most of the students understood (to borrow a phrase from Perry, 1970) that this was "the way They [the professors] want you to think," and many of them had mastered the procedure, but they preferred a more personal and empathic approach. For example, Priscilla said, "When I have an idea about something, and it differs from the way another person's thinking about it, I'll usually try to look at it from that person's point of view, see how they could say that, why they think they're right, why it makes sense." Now, when you play devil's advocate, you take a position contrary to the other person's, even when you agree with it, even when it seems intuitively right. Priscilla turns this upside down. She allies herself with the other person's position even when she disagrees with it. She is playing what Elbow calls the "believing game" (1973, 1986). Instead of looking for what's wrong with the other person's idea, she looks for why it makes sense, how it might be right, "saying Yes to it" (Elbow, 1986, p. 279).

Notice that Priscilla does not remain aloof from the other person. Connected knowing, like separate knowing, is "objective" in the sense that it too involves the suspension of one's own beliefs (or disbelief). But it is not impersonal or detached. Connected knowers do not operate from a neutral perspective; they adopt the perspective of a particular other: Priscilla tries to get behind the person's eyes, to "look at it from that person's point of view." This is what Elbow means by "believe." And Cecily says, "If you listen to people and listen to what they have to say, maybe you can understand why they feel the way they do. There are reasons. They're not just being irrational. When I read a philosopher, I try to think as the author does. It's hard, but I try not to bias the train of thought with my own impressions. I try to just pretend that I'm the author. I try to really just put myself in that person's place and feel why is it that they believe this way." The person with whom the connected knower empathizes need not be a real and present person. The connected knower takes a personal approach even to an impersonal thing like a philosophical argument, treating the text, as one student put it, "as if it were a friend."

Connected knowers believe that to understand what a person is saying, one must adopt the person's own terms. One must refrain from judgment. In this sense, connected knowing is uncritical. But it is not passive. It is a conscious procedure, requiring deliberation and effort. Cecily says, "I *try* to just pretend I'm the author." She says, "It's *hard*." But the effort in connected knowing is different from the effort required by separate knowing. In connected knowing, you do not try to impose a structure on the material you are trying to understand. You don't try to master the material or control it or transform it. You allow it to transform you. Elbow says that while the doubting game requires a "combative kind of energy that feels like clenching a muscle . . . the shape of the believing game is waiting, patience, not being in a hurry . . . [a] kind of trying-not-to-try" (1973, pp. 177, 180, 181).

Although connected knowing is uncritical, it is not unthinking. It may involve feeling; it always involves thinking. Connected knowers, like separate knowers, look beneath the surface. Cecily looks for "reasons" behind the other person's view. Priscilla wants to know how the person's position "makes sense," "why they think they're right." But the "reasons" connected knowers attempt to elicit are different from the reasons the separate knower looks for. Cecily does not demand that people support or justify their positions. She asks only that they tell her what in their experience led them to hold such a position. She wants to know the story, not the argument, behind the idea.

Constructed Knowing. We did not mean to imply, in *WWK*, that connected knowing was "better" than separate knowing. One procedure may be more effective in one context, the other in another. Although individuals may have stylistic predilections in one direction or the other, all students need to develop skill in both modes so that they can deploy whichever is appropriate on a given occasion. We know from research and from common observation that these procedures are not mutually exclusive; indeed, measures of the two appear to be orthogonal (David, 1999; Galotti, Drebus, and Reimer, 1999; Galotti and others, 1999). Ideally, we might even envision our students achieving a way of knowing that integrates the two procedures into one. In *WWK*, we called this perspective "constructed knowing." I describe the position more fully elsewhere (Clinchy, in press); here I offer only a brief sketch. Constructivists exhibit a sort of double vision. They use an approach that integrates the "active surrender" of connected knowing with the "mastery and control" of separate knowing. They move easily between the two modes, using each as a corrective to the other. Sara, a family therapist who is aware that she has a proclivity for connection, says, "If I find myself being too much into that close-up stance where I'm completely involved in that person's perspective and maybe lose touch with the professional stance, I need to scramble to get my professional stance back." Sara has evolved an approach that is simultaneously adversarial and empathic: she will "take an oppositional stance," voicing exceptions to a client's interpretations, but she phrases her comments in connected language, "in a way that hopefully isn't argumentative, but sort of like a confused statement." In the *WWK* sample and in subsequent research, we have found few traditional-aged undergraduates who describe a way of knowing as complex as Sara's, and in fact the development of full-blown constructed knowing may require experience beyond college. It is possible, though, that more undergraduates might achieve the perspective if connected knowing were more fully integrated into the goals and practices of higher education.

Connected Education

A "more connected education" would cultivate connections among students, between students and teachers, and between students and their work. (Clinchy, 1995; 1996; Stanton, 1996). Especially, perhaps, in our most "demanding" institutions, students rarely find the time to form intimate relationships with the material they are studying. One student confided, "I remember last semester getting *really* almost terrified when I was studying for finals, because all of a sudden I got so wrapped up in the material. . . . And I just realized, you know, that it was really exciting to do all this stuff. But if you did that all semester long, you'd go crazy. . . . It seems that you don't have a chance to reflect." In class, too, students need permission to reflect and to develop as well as defend ideas. They need to learn how to enter the perspectives of their classmates so that they can effectively think *with* (as well as *against*) them, increasing their skills in building on others' ideas and serving as midwives to each other's embryonic thoughts. They need teachers who are willing to share the *process* as well as the product of their thinking, teachers who are not afraid to think out loud and change their minds in public, teachers who ask "real questions" that invite students to say what they think rather than demonstrate what they know. Instead of dismissing students' accounts of personal experience with contempt as "anecdotal evidence," connected teachers treat them as a source of hypotheses, deserving to be nurtured.

Connected education requires more personal methods of assessing students' work: for example, longitudinal analysis of the development of each individual's performance over the course of the term, rather than a system in which students compete with each other and in which performance is measured in terms of an impersonal objective standard. The more separate system is useful for certification of the student's competence, but it is not clear that it serves any useful educational purpose. Indeed, anxiety about this form of evaluation can prevent students from becoming deeply involved in their work: they become outcome-oriented rather than process-oriented (Csikszentmihalyi, Rathunde, and Whalen, 1993); in time they often come to hate the process.

Elbow (1993) argues that teachers can help students form an attachment to their own writing by "saying Yes" to their essays, not by offering empty praise but by finding something genuinely valuable in it and helping the student see its value too. For both students and teachers, he says, attachment facilitates detachment: Teachers and students who find something to like in an essay will be more willing to invest energy in criticizing and revising it. In this more connected context, Simone might move toward constructed knowing. She might learn to write papers that she *and* the teacher liked, papers integrating well-founded arguments with "deep-founded beliefs" written not by "it" but by Simone herself.

References

Belenky, M. F., Clinchy, B. M., Goldberger, N. R., and Tarule, J. M. *Women's Ways of Knowing: The Development of Self, Mind, and Voice.* New York: Basic Books, 1997. (Originally published 1986.)

Bleich, D. "Sexism in Academic Styles of Learning." *Journal of Advanced Composition,* 1990, *10,* 231–247.

Clinchy, B. M. "A Connected Approach to the Teaching of Developmental Psychology." *Teaching of Psychology,* 1995, *22,* 100–104.

Clinchy, B. M. "Connected and Separate Knowing: Toward a Marriage of Two Minds." In N. R. Goldberger, J. M. Tarule, B. M. Clinchy, and M. F. Belenky (eds.), *Knowledge, Difference, and Power: Essays Inspired by* Women's Ways of Knowing. New York: Basic Books, 1996.

Clinchy, B. M., and Norem, J. K. (eds.). *Readings in Gender and Psychology.* New York: New York University Press, 1998.

Clinchy, B. M., and Zimmerman, C. "Epistemology and Agency in the Development of Undergraduate Women." In P. Perun (ed.), *The Undergraduate Woman: Issues in Educational Equity.* Lexington, Mass.: Heath, 1982.

Clinchy, B. M., and Zimmerman, C. "Growing Up Intellectually: Issues for College Women." *Work in Progress,* no. 19. Wellesley, Mass.: Stone Center Working Papers Series, 1985.

Csikszentmihalyi, M., Rathunde, K., and Whalen, S. *Talented Teenagers: The Roots of Success and Failure.* New York: Cambridge University Press, 1993.

David, C. J. "Fear of Success and Cognitive Styles in College Women." Unpublished undergraduate honors thesis, Wellesley College, 1999.

Elbow, P. "Appendix Essay: The Doubting Game and the Believing Game—An Analysis of the Intellectual Enterprise." In *Writing Without Teachers*. London: Oxford University Press, 1973.

Elbow, P. *Embracing Contraries*. New York: Oxford University Press, 1986.

Elbow, P. "Ranking, Evaluating, and Liking: Sorting Out Three Forms of Judgment." *College English*, 1993, 55, 187–206.

Galotti, K. M., Drebus, D. W., and Reimer, R. L. "Ways of Knowing as Learning Styles." Research display presented at the biennial meeting of the Society for Research in Child Development, Albuquerque, N.M., Apr. 1999.

Galotti, K. M., and others. "A New Way of Assessing Ways of Knowing: The Attitudes Toward Thinking and Learning Survey (ATTLS)." *Sex Roles*, 1999, 40, 745–766.

Perry, W. G., Jr. *Forms of Intellectual and Ethical Development in the College Years: A Scheme*. Austin, Tex.: Holt, Rinehart and Winston, 1970.

Rayman, P., and Brett, B. *Pathways for Women in Science: The Wellesley Report*. Wellesley, Mass.: Wellesley College, 1993.

Stanton, A. "Reconfiguring Teaching and Knowing in the College Classroom." In N. R. Goldberger, J. M. Tarule, B. M. Clinchy, and M. F. Belenky (eds.), *Knowledge, Difference, and Power: Essays Inspired by* Women's Ways of Knowing. New York: Basic Books, 1996.

BLYTHE MCVICKER CLINCHY is a professor in the Department of Psychology at Wellesley College in Wellesley, Massachusetts.

The author draws on the work of John Dewey, George Herbert Mead, and contemporary critical theorists to explore service learning's contribution to democratic citizenship. Central to the discussion is the author's concept of the "caring self."

Democratic Citizenship and Service Learning: Advancing the Caring Self

Robert A. Rhoads

The intent of this chapter is to advance research and theory on service learning and identity development. Specifically, I explore the concept of the "caring self," which I argue is vital to contemporary conceptions of teaching and learning. Defined in simplest terms, the caring self is *a sense of self firmly rooted in a concern for the well-being of others*. As I will argue, caring selves are crucial to a multicultural, democratic society.

Conceptions of democracy lie at the very heart of how we think about education and the teaching and learning processes we employ in working with college students. Consequently, throughout this chapter, I adopt an Aristotelian view of governance in which every member of a given society is believed to have the potential to influence public life and to become a caring and concerned citizen. In addition, a pragmatic assumption lies at the heart of my analysis: Colleges and universities exist in part to advance the social good. Although there are a variety of ways in which institutions of higher learning might contribute to the social good (advancing knowledge, economic development, community outreach, and so forth), one key contribution involves preparing students as concerned citizens through educational activities such as service learning.

In what follows, I discuss John Dewey's contribution to education and citizenship. I then link Dewey's vision of democratic citizenship with George Herbert Mead's work on the "social self," arguing that a democratic society thrives only when its citizens have a deep concern for others. I build upon the work of Dewey, Mead, and more contemporary critical and feminist theorists as I elaborate the caring self and introduce empirical research drawn from student participation in community service. I conclude by offering

NEW DIRECTIONS FOR TEACHING AND LEARNING, no. 82, Summer 2000   © Jossey-Bass Publishers

three key concerns to be addressed when developing service learning opportunities to promote the caring self.

Democracy and Education

The caring self is crucial to John Dewey's vision of democracy (1916), and education is a critical process in promoting active and caring citizenship. For example, Dewey believed that all knowledge should serve the well-being of society and that all citizens have the ability and obligation to participate in a variety of governance forms, ranging from national elections to neighborhood and community self-governance. Dewey's "New Education," with an emphasis on full participation by learners in the construction of knowledge, challenged what Harkavy and Benson described as the "uncompromisingly aristocratic and antidemocratic" foundations of Platonic thought, which "had perhaps its greatest (and most pernicious) impact on Western education" (1998, p. 12). They went on to describe the elitism inherent in Plato's philosophy: "Just as ideas were fixed and permanent for Plato, so too were society's classes and their characteristics. Knowledge could not be attained by the vast mass of people who did society's basic work. . . . True knowledge was the province of the ruling class, those few men capable of going beyond the sensate and material world to the external world of ideas" (p. 12).

For Dewey, democracy is something more than simply every citizen having the right to vote; democracy is a way of relational living in which the decisions and actions of one citizen must be understood in terms of their influence on the lives of others. From Dewey's perspective, democracy demands that citizens be knowledgeable of one another's lives and that they enter into decision-making processes that are collaborative and inclusive.

Dewey applied his vision of democracy to schooling, which he saw as the key social process in preparing democratic citizens. A democratic society depends on its citizens to engage in public life; without caring citizens, governance "by the people" cannot exist. For Dewey, education should mirror the forms of governance that give shape to the larger society.

Dewey saw an educated citizenry as more than a society of individuals with technical skills, vocational inclinations, and economic ambitions. And democracy is more than a political economy of free markets, competition, and entrepreneurship. A democracy also commands attention to volunteer agencies, churches, schools, and communities. It is dependent on interactive spheres of families, friends, acquaintances, and strangers, out of which often come the basis for public engagement or disengagement, social concern or apathy (Bellah and others, 1985). As Dewey noted, the essential work of democracy begins with communities and meaningful interactions: "There is no substitute for the vitality and depth of close and direct intercourse and attachment. . . . Democracy begins at home, and its home is the neighborly community" (1927, p. 213). Clearly, community lies at the heart of a vibrant democracy, and the work of Mead is helpful in connecting conceptions of community and self.

Mead's Social Self

Mead drew on the early work of Charles Horton Cooley (1902), who described the "looking-glass self," arguing that one's sense of self comes from the reflections others offer back to us. Mead advanced Cooley's thinking by identifying two structures at the core of the development of the self: the "I" and the "me." The "I" represents acting out a particular behavior: speaking, hitting a baseball, combing one's hair. The "me" relates to the sense one has about the "I," who is acting out a behavior or set of behaviors. The sense we develop about the "I" derives from the interpretations and reactions others offer to us (in Cooley's thinking, others provide a looking glass or mirror in which to see ourselves). We cannot develop an initial sense about ourselves without the help of others, who provide feedback and interact with the behaving "I." Through the thoughts of others, imagined by us and conceived through interactions with them, we envision ourselves as a "me," which becomes the object of our thoughts. "The self that answers to the 'me' arises out of the attitude of others to the individual," Mead stated in his 1914 lectures at the University of Chicago. He went on to add, "Our view of the self, so far as the form is concerned, is the individual as we conceive him to exist in the minds of other members of the group. This is the 'me.' The 'I' is the speaker over against the one spoken to, but the attention is given to the other. If we cannot turn the attention back to the self without taking the attitude of the other, we cannot immediately view ourselves" ([1914] 1982, p. 92).

Observing the "me" of the self involves taking the role of the other and imagining how we might appear, be interpreted, or be understood by someone else (we do this so frequently over the years that moving between the "I" and the "me" is practically a subconscious process). As Mead pointed out, "We are continually following up our own address to other persons by an understanding of what we are saying, and using that understanding in the direction of our continued speech. We are finding out what we are going to say, what we are going to do, by saying and doing, and in the process we are continually controlling the process itself" (1934, p. 140).

The idea of the "I" and the "me" interacting to form the self, which is both processual and fluid, can be confusing, yet at the same time it is absolutely basic to our experience as users of symbols. Allow me to offer an example. When a student makes an ill-conceived comment during a particular class, the student naturally imagines himself or herself through the eyes of others—in this case, through the eyes of other students and the professor in the same class. The student might even think, "That is me, whom I envision in my mind's eye, making a fool of myself!" This student might follow up an ill-advised comment with additional commentary designed to alter the images he or she believes others might have constructed. This very process of managing and constructing meaning was alluded to by a student when he was asked to discuss what he had learned as part of an intensive community service project: "I realized how much people learn by interpreting signals from others. It's so obvious in a situation like this—where you're working with people you hardly know. People learn so much without decisively learning it."

Obviously, social interaction is crucial to Mead's theory of the self: "It is impossible for the self to develop outside of social experience" (1934, p. 140). And as Schwalbe explained, "The thinking individual is thus thoroughly social; in fact, there could be no individual thought at all if not for the existence of communal life based on the creation and use of symbols" (1991, p. 283). Unless we can take the role of the other and view the "I" who is behaving as the "me," once it becomes the object of our gaze, we cannot develop a sense of self. Otherwise, we are only organisms acting without reflection (Blumer, 1969).

Mead's social self seems particularly helpful in understanding the service context. In fact, the kinds of reflections offered to students by fellow volunteers and by community members are likely to be positive sources of self-development. Thus if the community service project is structured properly (I will discuss this further in a later section), students experience an educational context that has much potential for fostering selves grounded in community-mindedness and caring.

In addition, the work of critical and feminist theorists reminds us of the need to foster caring and concerned students. For example, Giroux (1992) argues that a concern for democratic ethics ought to be at the center of pedagogy: "Ethics becomes a practice that broadly connotes one's personal and social sense of responsibility to the Other. Thus, ethics is taken up as a struggle against inequality and as a discourse for expanding basic human rights" (p. 74). And Noddings (1984) contends that moral education involves building caring relationships through a deep exploration of otherness: "When we see the other's reality as a possibility for us, we must act to eliminate the intolerable, to reduce the pain, to fill the need, to actualize the dream. When I am in this sort of relationship with another, when the other's reality becomes a real possibility for me, I care" (p. 14).

Building on the work of Mead, Dewey, and contemporary critical scholars, several years ago I began to think of service-related identity exploration in terms of the "caring self." Consequently, from 1991 to 1997 I collected ethnographic data about student participation in community service, both during weeklong intensive projects as well as ongoing service projects in home and university communities (see Rhoads, 1997, 1998, for a more extensive discussion of method). In what follows, I specifically focus on the caring self as I offer some empirical data to help make sense of the concept and its importance.

Service and the Caring Self

The basic rationale for the need for caring selves is rooted in a simple but important assertion offered by King and Baxter Magolda: "How individuals construct knowledge and use their knowledge is closely tied to their sense of self" (1996, p. 166). Thus if we want students to assume active roles in society based on an attitude of care and concern for others, we need to help students foster a caring sense of self. The challenge then is to create educational contexts where caring is a vital component. When caring becomes central to how we educate our students, identities rooted in caring and a concern for others are more likely to emerge.

In symbolic interactionist terms, when a student engages in service for (ideally, with) others, particular kinds of social interactions are likely to occur that contribute to one's self-definition as a concerned citizen and a caring person. Listen to two students talk about the self-exploration that took place as part of their community service work:

"Volunteer work is one of the things I've made time for as part of my own struggle to figure out what's important to me. It helps me figure out the kind of person I am going to be. I don't want to do things only for me. I want to help others and contribute to someone else's life if I can."

"I got involved with a lot of self-esteem work, primarily with teenagers. It helped me think more seriously about my understanding of myself and how others think of me. I began to wonder about what kind of person I was. I began to ask questions of myself."

These students highlight how community service offers experientially based learning that fosters self-analysis. Relatedly, community service often challenges commonly held beliefs about what it means to be a successful person. For example, a student who worked with homeless citizens in Washington, D.C., commented, "We pass the time without really questioning our lives. The people of the streets have challenged me."

Another student noted that she participated in community service work because she felt an obligation to her community. She believed that service provides an opportunity to escape "self-centered" behavior and "step outside" of herself for a while. The irony of her point is telling: In seeking to move beyond self-centered behavior and step outside of herself through giving and interacting with others (indeed, focusing on others), she achieved a deeper understanding of herself. In the end, she served not only her community but her own development as well.

Because of the value service learning places on student involvement in communities, it also models the kinds of caring and committed lives needed for democracy to thrive. The following students offer insights into various thoughts and interactions about the meaning of community often inspired by service projects. All three students were participants in a weeklong community service project on Johns Island, South Carolina:

"I always try to be independent, and it was beneficial for me to have to lean on others during the week. Our world has become too individualistic, and this experience has helped remind me that community is the answer."

"The people of Johns Island may not have an elm-lined street, but it's a real community because they care for each other. They have that, and maybe that's something we can take with us—talking with our neighbors and giving to them."

"What you define as your community is important to each individual, because everybody sees their community in a different way and therefore it is important to know when you are overstepping your bounds—when you might be imposing your value system on someone else. It's hard to determine. Whose community is it? How you define the limits of your community affects what you feel comfortable doing."

Thoughts about the meaning of community do not derive solely from the interactions students have with community members; issues involving the meaning and power of community may emerge from a group of student volunteers as well. As one student explained, "I need to be in community with people who are interested in radical social change. Together we can work and witness all kinds of changes and perhaps come closer to finding some answers." A second student added, "There is an enormous sense of hope generated by twenty other volunteers working together for the same social cause. This hope is fuel for my own personal fire, which drives me to work on behalf of those less privileged."

Organizing Service to Promote the Caring Self

A central facet of my study of student involvement in service focused on aspects of the service context key to challenging a student's sense of self and ultimately promoting a more caring self. I identify three components that have practical implications for how we think about the structure of service learning: mutuality, personalization, and reflection.

Mutuality demands that all parties have a say in the way service projects are structured, including identifying various needs to be met. Too often college- and university-initiated projects reflect patronizing strategies in which the institution believes it knows what is best for the community. Mutuality also reminds us that both the "doers" and the "done to" (borrowing terms from Radest, 1993) give and receive. Very seldom do we prepare students for the gifts (positive feelings reflected back to them) that come with service, and quite often they express feelings of guilt for such rewards. Students need to learn that "giving requires receiving," as one young woman who worked with homeless citizens in D.C. noted. Thus mutuality promotes the caring self by situating all parties as equals and all parties as potential "givers" and "receivers."

Another key aspect of a successful service project promotes personalized interactions between students and community members with whom a service is rendered. Time and time again, students made a point of how valuable the personal interactions were during their service projects. There is a huge difference between sorting shoes at a shoe bank and never meeting the children and families who use the service and actually having the opportunity to interact with them. Similarly, building a house for Habitat for Humanity alongside the family who will eventually move in to it is quite different from a construction project in which the prospective family remains unseen and unknown. Personalized interactions contribute to the caring self because such interactions challenge students to explore "otherness," which is vital to a self rooted in a concern for others.

By reflection, I refer to various activities built into a service project that direct time and attention toward the meaning and significance of the experience. Reflection may come in a variety of forms, including small group discussions, integrative group projects, reflective writing projects such as journals, or group skits. The point is that reflection gives students the opportunity to think about and conceptualize the service experience. Such opportunities enable students to make connections among all aspects of their academic and personal lives, which are too often disconnected by academic structures (the formal curriculum and the cocurriculum). Hence reflection is key to promoting the caring self because it forces students to give serious thought to their service experience and their overall lives.

Conclusion

As our society grows increasingly diverse, we need citizens who embrace otherness as part of a caring and concerned sense of self. The caring self presents opposition to widespread xenophobia, so common in today's complex and multiplicitous society (indeed, the "generalized other" becomes multiplicitous in a postmodern, multicultural world). As Mead reminds us, it is within the context of community that selves emerge, and thus pedagogical strategies such as service learning offer intense and extended opportunities for students to develop caring selves.

The concepts of mutuality, personalization, and reflection are consistent with democratic, constructivist views of teaching and learning. Mutuality challenges us to give serious thought to egalitarian service projects in that all parties must be part of the decision making, as well as the giving and the receiving. Personalization demands that students engage in service interactions in which their personal worlds intersect with the worlds of others. This important intersection helps students see how social life is interwoven and how together we might arrive at jointly constructed conceptions of community. Reflection reminds us that deep change demands the time and energy of serious thought. All of these components make service learning a viable pedagogy for advancing democratic citizenship in the academy.

References

Bellah, R. N., and others. *Habits of the Heart: Individualism and Commitment in American Life*. New York: HarperCollins, 1985.

Blumer, H. *Symbolic Interactionism: Perspective and Method*. Berkeley: University of California Press, 1969.

Cooley, C. H. *Human Nature and the Social Order*. New York: Scribner, 1902.

Dewey, J. *Democracy and Education*. New York: Macmillan, 1916.

Dewey, J. *The Public and Its Problems*. New York: Henry Holt, 1927.

Giroux, H. *Border Crossings: Cultural Workers and the Politics of Education*. New York: Routledge, 1992.

Harkavy, I., and Benson, L. "De-Platonizing and Democratizing Education as the Bases of Service Learning." In R. A. Rhoads and J.P.F. Howard (eds.), *Academic Service Learning: A Pedagogy of Action and Reflection*. New Directions for Teaching and Learning, no. 73. San Francisco: Jossey-Bass, 1998.

King, P. M., and Baxter Magolda, M. B. "A Developmental Perspective on Learning." *Journal of College Student Development*, 1996, 37, 163–173.

Mead, G. H. *Mind, Self, and Society* (ed. C. W. Morris). Chicago: University of Chicago Press, 1934.

Mead, G. H. *The Individual and the Social Self* (ed. D. L. Miller). Chicago: University of Chicago Press, 1982. (Originally published 1914.)

Noddings, N. *Caring: A Feminine Approach to Ethics and Moral Education*. Berkeley: University of California Press, 1984.

Radest, H. *Community Service: Encounter with Strangers*. Westport, Conn.: Praeger, 1993.

Rhoads, R. A. *Community Service and Higher Learning: Explorations of the Caring Self*. Albany: State University of New York Press, 1997.

Rhoads, R. A. "In the Service of Citizenship: A Study of Student Involvement in Community Service." *Journal of Higher Education*, 1998, 69, 277–297.

Schwalbe, M. L. "Social Structure and the Moral Self." In J. A. Howard and P. L. Callero (eds.), *The Self-Society Dynamic: Cognition, Emotion, and Action*. Cambridge: Cambridge University Press, 1991.

ROBERT A. RHOADS *is an associate professor in the Department of Educational Administration at Michigan State University in East Lansing.*

*How African American and white students and faculty
develop a strong identity and healthy interpersonal
relationships is explored. Faculty are encouraged to
engage students in dialogue about multicultural issues
and adapt their teaching practices to create a culturally
responsive learning environment for students and faculty.*

Creating a Culturally Responsive Learning Environment for African American Students

Mary F. Howard-Hamilton

"All students, including those from traditional White, middle class backgrounds, have a right to expect that their courses present comprehensive knowledge and prepare them to succeed in a multicultural community. Understanding the perspectives of many groups enriches the lives of all students, and promotes a more equitable society for all" (Kitano, 1997a, p. 4).

Faculty members have the power to make the learning environment for all students inclusive and supportive rather than isolating and exclusionary. This can be done successfully by creating a culturally responsive curriculum in which the life experiences of diverse groups will not be expunged from the course content. Students' ability to understand multiple perspectives is mediated by, among other factors, their own racial identity development. Theories of racial identity development, for both people of color and whites, can help us understand this important dimension of preparing all students to succeed in a multicultural society.

Racial identity theories have been developed to understand how white people and individuals from visible racial ethnic groups identify with their racial cohorts (Carter, 1995). As children grow and develop in this society, they become aware that they belong to a specific racial group. According to Carter, "the challenge for each individual is to incorporate race into his or her personal identity" (p. 82). Specifically, an individual's identity and personality is complex and dynamic, made up of immutable characteristics, unusual experiences, and personal challenges and choices. Personalities and identities are also products of societal influences such as the family, the church, political processes, and schools (Robinson and Howard-Hamilton, 2000).

Educational institutions perpetuate gender-role socialization as well as racial and cultural stereotyping through the hidden curriculum (Jones and Young, 1997; Sadker and Sadker, 1994) and banking education (Freire, 1970). The hidden curriculum is a covert and subliminal teaching and learning thought process that "works to both perpetuate power relationships, cultural hegemony, and political relationships and to impede the progress of those without the ability to identify and understand its existence" (Jones and Young, 1997, p. 93). Moreover, the classroom is controlled by the instructor who chooses to teach only traditional material that reflects the successes of the dominant society. This teaching method is further exacerbated by the banking education process. Freire (1970) notes that "banking education anesthetizes and inhibits creative power" (p. 68) by the instructors' depositing information that they perceive is "right" and "the students patiently receive, memorize, and repeat" (p. 58) this material on exams. Often students regard the teacher's knowledge as universally correct; thus stereotypes could be internalized by students without any challenge.

To understand the African American student's meaning-making and learning process in the classroom, it is important to understand who the student is and what that student believes in, as well as the identity construction of the instructor. It is imperative that faculty use racial identity theory to understand the psychological and cognitive complexities of the diverse students they teach to make the classroom learning process a liberatory practice for everyone. Helms and Cook (1999) state that the theories and models are "pathways for overcoming internalized racism and achieving a healthy socioracial self-conception under varying conditions of racial oppression" (p. 81).

Racial Identity Theories

The theories presented provide a rough map or diagram of a developmental pilgrimage from an identity that is steeped in racial biases and prejudice to an identity that is affirming of others and emancipated from racism (Helms and Cook, 1999; Ponterotto, Casas, Suzuki, and Alexander, 1995; Robinson and Howard-Hamilton, 2000). When faculty members understand the student's racial identity process, they may become more comfortable and less threatened "by the strength and variety of student attitudes as well as their heightened emotions as they react to cultural issues" (Wlodkowski and Ginsberg, 1995, p. 51). This allows a developmental process to take place for both the faculty member and the student that is based on mutual respect for differences, dialogue, and continuous reflection.

One framework for understanding students' racial identity processes is the Minority Identity Development (MID) model (Atkinson, Morten, and Sue, 1993). The MID involves a five-stage process to positive racial identity development. According to the authors, the MID is applicable to all visible racial or ethnic groups. The first stage is *conformity,* in which the individual internalizes attitudes that reflect preferences for the dominant race and negative attitudes that reflect preferences for one's own race and culture. *Dissonance,* the second stage, evokes feelings and attitudes that reflect racial-cultural confusion and conflict. In the third stage, *resistance,* individuals find themselves rejecting the dominant culture's values and embracing their cultural group of origin. In the penultimate stage, *introspection,* there is a period of reflection in which the values of the dominant and personal cultural groups are evaluated. The final stage, *awareness,* finds the individuals engulfed in a sense of self-fulfillment as the confusion and conflict from the previous stages are resolved.

A similar racial identity developmental process is described in the Nigrescence or Negro-to-Black Conversion Model for African Americans (Cross, 1991). Cross indicates that there are five stages of identity maturation and responsiveness to others. The stages are described along with examples of students' responses to teaching and learning at each level:

1. *Pre-Encounter.* There is an identification with the dominant (white) culture and rejection or denial of any connection with African American people and culture. At this stage, the student may not contribute significantly to classroom discussion; a student may make a comment such as "I have been quiet in class, but it is because I agree with what people are saying and I don't want them to think that I am different."

2. *Encounter.* The student begins an African American consciousness-raising effort in this stage because of a traumatic encounter with the dominant (white) culture. This trauma may occur as early as the first day in a predominantly white class because of the stereotype threat (Steele, 1999), which is the fear of being "viewed through the lens of a negative stereotype, or the fear of doing something that would inadvertently confirm that stereotype" (p. 46). After receiving a poor grade on a paper, a student might say, "I can't believe I received a D because I got excellent marks in my advanced placement classes in high school. I talked to the instructor, and she asked me where I was from and what my ACT score was. She said most students like me do not have the basic writing skills to get an A in her class. I was so angry, I just walked out." This student has been stereotyped as below average in intelligence by the instructor's socialized belief system. The student's self-confidence has been shattered, and now the student is fearful that others have the same perception.

3. *Immersion-Emersion.* The student becomes intently interested in learning more about the African American culture. There is an in-depth immersion into the history of the culture and negating everything learned about the dominant (white) culture. As a student learns more about African Americans, a comment like this may be heard: "I am going to change my major to ethnic studies because the stuff I am learning now does not interest

me at all. I am tired of being around white students all day. I don't know whether or not I like this place any longer."

4. *Internalization.* The student embodies a strong African American identity and transcends the psychological impact of racism. Resolving these issues, the student may say, "I cannot get angry at the teacher for not singing my song or talking about my culture in class; I have to sing my own song and share that with others. Maybe the projects I write will help the teacher understand my culture."

5. *Internalization-Commitment.* The student maintains an empowered African American identity while resisting the various forms of social oppression. At this stage, the student has developed a healthy psychological resistance to negative caricatures of his or her race or culture, and the end result is liberation and empowerment (Howard-Hamilton, 1997; Robinson and Howard-Hamilton, 1994). A student may comment, "School has been a struggle at times because I felt so isolated. I really want to help others so they will know that they can make it if there is some support."

A similar psychosocial developmental trajectory occurs in the White Racial Identity Ego Statuses Model (Helms and Cook, 1999), a seven-status process of overcoming internalized racism for whites. The statuses are divided into two phases: (1) the abdication of a racist identity ("contact through reintegration") and (2) the creation of a nonracist white identity ("immersion through autonomy") (Carter, 1995). When evolving through the statuses, the white person is attempting to replace socialized messages and beliefs of entitlement and privilege with a "nonracist and realistic self-affirming collective (racial) identity" (Helms and Cook, 1999, p. 89). The seven statuses are described next, illustrated in the context of an instructor's perspectives across this trajectory.

1. *Contact.* Contentment with racial status quo and insensitivity to racism and one's contribution to it. An example of this status is evident in an instructor's view of her syllabus: "I don't think I need to revise my literature syllabus to include African American writers because many passages in the classics do include references about people of color."

2. *Disintegration.* Confusion and distress when facing racial moral dilemmas that force one to take sides between own-group loyalty and humanism. The instructor comments that "this is everyone's literature class, not just mine. The students should know that this is American literature. I get so upset when they want to read about one ethnic group by one ethnic writer."

3. *Reintegration.* Glorified ideals of one's socioracial group and vilification of and prejudicial attitudes toward other groups. The instructor defends her syllabus by stating, "It's not my fault that the African American writers were ignored in the past and their materials were not part of the mainstream canon. I am not responsible for their misfortunes."

4. *Pseudo-Independence.* "Intellectualized commitment to one's own socioracial group and subtle superiority and tolerance of other socioracial groups as long as they can be helped to conform to white standards of merit" (Helms and Cook, 1999, p. 92). The instructor comments, "Reading a course syllabus by my colleague who teaches literature at Prestigious University, I realize that there are a few good books written by people of color that may enhance my class discussions."

5. *Immersion.* The search for a new and compassionate definition of being white and an attempt to debunk racist stereotypes and seek accurate information about racial ethnic groups, racism, and privilege. As a researcher, the instructor comments, "Perhaps it is time for me to reassess my perspective on literature and view what the white writers are saying about diverse groups. This may help me intellectually understand how my students perceive the literature as well."

6. *Emersion.* A sense of appreciation and group solidarity and pride that accompanies being with other white people who are seeking new self-knowledge. The instructor thanks her colleague at Prestigious University for sharing the course syllabus and is engaged in a dialogue about infusing new material into her curriculum. The process of grappling with racial discrimination and personal prejudice has been emotionally draining and overwhelming at times, but the conversation with other colleagues helps immeasurably.

7. *Autonomy.* An affirming and informed socioracial-group commitment and adoption of personal standards to prevent and avoid contributing to racial oppression. The instructor has decided, "I am revamping my course syllabus to include multiple perspectives by racially diverse writers. Discussions may be challenging for everyone, but at least my semester won't be boring!"

The establishment of a nonracist white identity is an important component to developing rapport with people of color. "A person's worldview, through the lens of racial identity, has implications for how he or she processes information, forms perceptions, understands behavior, and selects and understands what is important" (Carter, 1995, p. 113). The instructor should have a personal appreciation of the concept of culture and racial identity (Ponterotto, Casas, Suzuki, and Alexander, 1995). A faculty member can covertly thwart the intellectual learning process for a student of color if there is a stereotypical perception of that person's abilities. If students of color feel empowered, respected, and connected with the people in the learning environment, they develop a capacity to concentrate; thus thinking is significantly enhanced (Kitano, 1997b; Wlodkowski and Ginsberg, 1995). It is important to emphasize the point that white students engage in the same process of racial identity formation and development as students of color.

Effective Dialogue and Teaching Practices

There are three levels of course change that can be correlated with White Racial Identity Consciousness. Kitano (1997b) notes that level 1 is an exclusive course that "presents and maintains traditional, mainstream experiences and perspectives on the discipline. If alternative perspectives are included, they are selected to confirm stereotypes" (p. 23). This level can be correlated to the White Racial Identity Ego Statuses of contact, disintegration, and reintegration, in which the instructor maintains a banking education philosophy and integrates a hidden curriculum. Information is exchanged in a didactic manner, objective or subjective written exams are used exclusively, and conversations and dialogue are controlled or directed by the instructor. It is important to note that African American students could be at the pre-encounter or encounter stage of Nigrescence and are experiencing extreme discomfort and sensing that their voices are not being heard. This environment could be frustrating and lead to student-teacher hostility.

A second level is an inclusive course change process that "presents traditional views but adds alternative perspectives" (Kitano, 1997b, p. 23). These perspectives and new viewpoints may be dispersed within the curriculum "without elaboration to efforts at analyzing and understanding reasons for historical exclusion" (p. 23). This level can be correlated with Helms and Cook's pseudo-independence and immersion statuses of White Racial Identity Consciousness because there is some questioning whether or not it is appropriate to continue to exclude the voices of underrepresented groups from the curriculum. The African American students are keenly aware that there is not a true commitment to the curricular revisions and note that the teacher is taking a patronizing view of historical inclusion. The African American students are at the encounter stage leading into immersion-emersion.

The third level, transformed, embraces the emersion and autonomy statuses of Helms and Cook's model. The instructor is attempting to challenge the students to think globally about diversity issues. Furthermore, "a transformed course challenges traditional views and assumptions; encourages new ways of thinking; and reconceptualizes the field in light of new knowledge, scholarship, and ways of knowing (Kitano, 1997b, p. 23). At this level, instructor privilege and power are dismantled with the banking education model abandoned for a teaching method that encourages self-evaluation and reflection. The instructor also includes class projects that engender the personal transformation process and reflect real-life issues. The African American students are becoming engaged in the course content and beginning to take part in the class dialogue. The students leave the class with a sense of internalized pride and understanding as well as respect for the values of diverse groups. The third level is where all parties, students and faculty, should be to maintain a culturally responsive curriculum.

Designing a curriculum that is culturally responsive should include the following norms (Wlodkowski and Ginsberg, 1995):

1. Coursework that emphasizes a connection to human need or interest so that the students can feel a part of something that is relevant to them
2. Teachers who are collaborative with the learners by helping them understand the creation of meaning and the virtue of their own thinking
3. Students working together as a community of learners
4. Students and instructor assuming a blame-free and trusting belief in people and their potential to be transformed
5. Students being treated equally in the classroom and invited to address behaviors, practices, or policies that are prejudicial

The redesign of the curriculum also requires heightened white racial identity consciousness because there may be more flexibility and creativity for new activities at the higher statuses. A person in the early statuses would be resistant to change, may blame the students of color for not being able to persist, and may stereotype them as a group of underachievers.

There are several instructional methods and techniques, as well as learning activities and projects, that can create a culturally responsive classroom for all students. First, the instructor must be willing to empower students and be comfortable with the disagreements that come with extensive dialogue, which inevitably leads to dissonance. The teacher should not get defensive or ignore or demean students' questions. Instead, an infusion of diverse perspectives should be intertwined in the curriculum. This will encourage all learners to read about diverse perspectives and not just material from the African American or white worldview. Carter and Wilson (1994) found that the most significant factor in retaining students of color on college campuses is the quality of interaction they have with faculty members. All the more reason to abandon the hidden curriculum and banking education concept because students and faculty can learn from each other if there is reciprocal communication.

Students should be allowed to engage in self-exploration through journal writing and through raising and answering their own questions. Such activities encourage them to find their own voices and make meaning of the classroom learning process for themselves. Again, the instructor should be comfortable with affective dialogue when students vent frustration, anger, guilt, and shame when delving into issues of racial consciousness. Class activities should provide opportunities for students to share their knowledge about perseverance and cultural awareness outside the classroom (as in the case of service learning)—to a group of high school students, for example, who may be experiencing difficulty with authority figures or who lack racial or ethnic role models. The instructor should also interweave small group tasks to encourage dialogue as well as raise the students' confidence level. Case study discussions in small groups can evoke moral dilemma decision-making and group consensus processes, which lead to higher-level listening skills and multiple perspective taking. Faculty should encourage students to work in study groups to share various perceptions of their reading and to prepare for exams.

The instructor should revise the course syllabus to include reading selections that have a multicultural perspective. This could be accomplished by providing a supplemental reading list and selecting texts that treat women and people of color as an integral part of the book rather than as an addendum. The syllabus should speak to the instructor's educational beliefs and teaching philosophy and the learning process in the classroom. This will set the tone for being respectful when hearing a person's story and understanding that the learning process is a two-way street; it is not the responsibility of the teacher to deposit information. Last, instead of a review of faculty performance, have students complete an instructor-designed end-of-semester class evaluation that reflects how the content and instruction might be improved (Kitano, 1997b). This empowers students to take part in transforming the curriculum to be more inclusive and sensitive to hearing the voices of underrepresented groups.

Conclusion

Recognizing the diverse and unique backgrounds of all students in the classroom enhances the learning experience for everyone. Interactions with students who are from different racial and ethnic backgrounds helps people acquire more accurate values and views about the systems that govern our lives. Discrimination, prejudice, and racism reduce opportunities for many African American students. Consciously and unconsciously, these biases are present in the classroom environment, and faculty should recognize that their own racial identity development and responsive teaching methods are key factors in reducing prejudice in our society.

References

Atkinson, D. R., Morten, G., and Sue, D. W. *Counseling American Minorities: A Cross-Cultural Perspective.* (4th ed.) Dubuque, Iowa: Brown and Benchmark, 1993.

Carter, D. J., and Wilson, R. *Minorities in Higher Education, 1993: Twelfth Annual Status Report.* Washington, D.C.: American Council on Education, 1994.

Carter, R. T. *The Influence of Race and Racial Identity in Psychotherapy: Toward a Racially Inclusive Model.* New York: Wiley, 1995.

Cross, W. E. *Shades of Black: Diversity in African American Identity.* Philadelphia: Temple University Press, 1991.

Freire, P. *Pedagogy of the Oppressed.* New York: Continuum, 1970.

Helms, J. E., and Cook, D. A. *Using Race and Culture in Counseling and Psychotherapy: Theory and Process.* Needham Heights, Mass.: Allyn & Bacon, 1999.

Howard-Hamilton, M. F. "Theory to Practice: Applying Developmental Theories Relevant to African American Men." In M. J. Cuyjet (ed.), *Helping African American Men Succeed in College.* New Directions for Student Services, no. 80. San Francisco: Jossey-Bass, 1997.

Jones, T., and Young, G. A. "Classroom Dynamics: Disclosing the Hidden Curriculum." In A. I. Morey and M. K. Kitano (eds.), *Multicultural Course Transformation in Higher Education: A Broader Truth.* Needham Heights, Mass.: Allyn & Bacon, 1997.

Kitano, M. K. "A Rationale and Framework for Course Change." In A. I. Morey and M. K. Kitano (eds.), *Multicultural Course Transformation in Higher Education: A Broader Truth.* Needham Heights, Mass.: Allyn & Bacon, 1997a.

Kitano, M. K. "What a Course Will Look Like After Multicultural Change." In A. I. Morey and M. K. Kitano (eds.), *Multicultural Course Transformation in Higher Education: A Broader Truth*. Needham Heights, Mass.: Allyn & Bacon, 1997b.

Ponterotto, J. G., Casas, J. M., Suzuki, L. A., and Alexander, C. M. *Handbook of Multicultural Counseling*. Thousand Oaks, Calif.: Sage, 1995.

Robinson, T. L., and Howard-Hamilton, M. F. "An Afrocentric Paradigm: Foundation for a Healthy Self-Image and Healthy Interpersonal Relationships." *Journal of Mental Health Counseling*, 1994, *16*, 327–339.

Robinson, T. L., and Howard-Hamilton, M. F. *The Convergence of Race, Ethnicity, and Gender: Multiple Identities in Counseling*. Upper Saddle River, N.J.: Merrill/Prentice Hall, 2000.

Sadker, M., and Sadker, D. *Failing at Fairness: How America's Schools Cheat Girls*. New York: Scribner, 1994.

Steele, C. M. "Thin Ice 'Stereotype Threat' and Black College Students." *Atlantic*, Aug. 1999, pp. 44–54.

Wlodkowski, R. J., and Ginsberg, M. B. *Diversity and Motivation: Culturally Responsive Teaching*. San Francisco: Jossey-Bass, 1995.

MARY F. HOWARD-HAMILTON *is an associate professor and coordinator of the Student Personnel in Higher Education Program in the Department of Educational Leadership, Policy, and Foundations at the University of Florida, Gainesville.*

High-ability black college students face the often daunting task of blending their academic interest and racial affiliation into their sense of self. This chapter focuses on the challenges in integrating these factors and the influence of interactions with peers and with faculty.

Identity Development of High-Ability Black Collegians

Sharon Fries-Britt

The study of black students and their academic, social, and psychological experiences in the academy has increased significantly in the past four decades. As black students gained access to predominantly white institutions in the United States, their presence underscored significant differences and needs relative to white students. Research on the academic and social factors affecting black students (Allen, 1981; Fleming, 1984; Nettles, Theony, and Gosman; 1986; Pascarella and Terenzini, 1991; Sedlacek, 1987) provided knowledge that was used to enhance students' development and to improve learning environments in and outside of the classroom.

Studying smaller and distinct populations of students can provide tremendous insight into how students learn and how to create environments to improve their intellectual development. As we aspire to find ways to improve teaching practices and learning outcomes for all students, we must understand the various ways that students are shaped by their experiences prior to and during the college years. As we understand more of the influences that shape their lives, we begin to understand how to create intersections in our teaching and in the learning process that allow students to become fully engaged in learning. My observations in this chapter are informed by extensive interviews conducted with twelve high-achieving black students who were enrolled from 1990 to 1994 in a merit-based scholarship program for students in math, science, and engineering (the Meyerhoff Scholars at the University of Maryland, Baltimore County, UMBC). Established in 1989, the Meyerhoff program is a nationally recognized program serving high-achieving African Americans in math and science. To become a Meyerhoff, students must maintain a B average or better and have

NEW DIRECTIONS FOR TEACHING AND LEARNING, no. 82, Summer 2000   © Jossey-Bass Publishers

outstanding SAT scores. For more details about the program see Hrabowski, Maton, and Greif (1998).

The students' voices in this chapter bridge a gap for a segment of the black student population we know little about—academically talented black collegians. This chapter explores one perspective on identity development: the blending of ability and race in a select group of high-ability black collegians. These students' experiences reveal a complex process over time where one's sense of self as a learner is shaped by cognitive, intrapersonal, and interpersonal development. Their interactions with teachers, peers, and others impede or enhance their ability to blend their racial and intellectual selves. Faculty must understand the important role of racial identity development in the learning process and how it interfaces with other identity issues like intellectual development to cultivate a strong sense of self.

Academically talented students are, almost by definition, naturally attracted to the learning process. However, black students (and other students) may encounter barriers on campus that detract from their learning. Some external barriers stem from the institutional climate. Recently, Hurtado and others (1999) identified campus barriers, including the historical legacy of a campus, structural diversity (actual numbers of minority students and faculty), psychological climate, and behavioral dimensions of campus climate. Other barriers result from internal struggles that black students face as they encounter various levels of racial consciousness (Cross, 1991) and as they develop a sense of self over time. Learning more about the barriers to student learning enables us to construct stronger intellectual pathways for students, moving us closer to creating successful academic experiences for all students. While we have come to understand much more about the academic and social needs of black students, we must pay more attention to how black students learn and to factors that inspire and encourage them to develop intellectually. Understanding how to cultivate and enhance their development in the classroom and learning more about what makes a difference in formal and informal interactions is the challenge. The insights and experiences of the students in this chapter are used to recommend conditions that promote and cultivate learning for some black students (and students in general).

The Challenges of Blending an Academic and Racial Identity

Two essential components emerged as important to students' establishing a sense of self—academic ability and racial affiliation. Both factors were significant in the experiences that students shared about interactions with peers, the broader community, and faculty. Consequently, both influenced how they connected to and interacted with others. Their stories reveal a change in perspective about their sense of "academic" self and "racial" self over time. Their confidence and ability to blend their intellectual and racial self was enhanced as they encountered more peers like themselves and environments that supported their interests. The reassurance and ease they experienced in a community of "like-type" peers later in college suggests a developmental change in their sense of identity from earlier experiences with peers in junior high and high school. How academic and racial experiences contributed to the larger picture of self is evidenced in their narratives.

High-achieving black students must master a baffling balancing act that they experience as they manage their intellectual ability. On the one hand, they find it necessary to conceal their intelligence, yet on the other hand, they feel that they have to go out of their way to prove that they are smart. Often the pressure to prove that they are capable is not just for personal reasons; as members of the extended black community, they feel a responsibility to prove that blacks in general are intelligent.

The reasons for concealing intelligence vary. One male student said, "In high school, if you had the grades, you kind of kept it quiet because you didn't want to be accused of being a nerd and not being in the in crowd, which didn't study or come to school half the time." Not being in the "in crowd" or being perceived as a "nerd" is often at the core of what causes students to camouflage their academic ability. For high-ability black students, this is compounded by their desire to fit into the community of their black peers. Ford (1996) emphasized the importance of the peer group for students in gifted programs. She observed that "once placed in gifted programs, Black students make numerous social sacrifices and take many risks. They risk, for example, rejection from Black peers, who may perceive gifted Black students as being untrue to their cultural and racial group; they risk isolation and alienation from White peers in the gifted program who do not understand Black students; they risk being under the guidance of teachers who do not understand them" (p. 79).

Evidence of peer rejection is well documented in the literature (Cooley, Cornell, and Lee, 1991; Fordham and Ogbu, 1986; Lindstrom and Van Sant, 1986). Because intelligence has been generally associated with whites, many minority youth perceive good grades and interest in academics as "acting white" (Fordham and Ogbu, 1986); consequently, black students who do well academically may be resistant to demonstrating their ability in the classroom.

Sometimes the cover-up of academic ability stems from the actions of authority figures. It is not unusual for high-ability students to give accounts of experiences early in their education where they felt unsupported. One student provided examples of several incidents early in her schooling where her parents constantly had to confront the issue of her grades with her teachers. This student provided these observations as a backdrop to explaining how, throughout her life, she had to deal with issues of racism and people not accepting her academic talent as a black student.

Then there was first grade. Mrs. Stern was a math teacher. For some reason she wanted to keep giving me Bs when I earned As. My parents had to have a little chat with these folks, and that got straightened out and I got shifted to a higher-level class. In the second grade, Ms. Smith, social science, wanted to give me a C when I had earned an A, and [that led to] another meeting with my parents and Ms. Smith and the headmaster, and my mom caught Ms. Smith trying to change one of my grades in the grade book so it would look justified, right there in front of the headmaster.

Minority gifted students are likely to experience difficulties in school environments (Olszewski-Kubilius and Scott, 1992). Teachers and other school officials have been inadequate in identifying gifted minority students (Serwatka, Deering, and Stoddard, 1989). Influenced by larger social images of who makes up the intellectual elite, many have dismissed minorities outright. Fortunately, this student's parents were actively involved in the student's academic life and were able to intervene very quickly. The student was able to maintain a high sense of esteem and apprehension of her academic strength because she had the support of parents who recognized her academic ability and were concerned about the teacher's evaluation.

At the other end of the spectrum, some students have a strong desire to demonstrate academic ability. This usually happens as a result of incidents involving students of another race (primarily white students) who challenge the competence of high-ability black students or express concern that they receive special treatment because of race rather than ability. Several of the students I interviewed expressed frustration in dealing with these attitudes. Although annoyed, they were not completely surprised and actually felt that these comments motivated them to achieve more. One student explained, "The Caucasian students have mentioned to us that, you know, it's no big deal that we are in the scholarship program, because they basically just give black students money for no reason. I mean, that's what it seems to us because when they come to us, they're always saying, 'Oh well, I could not have gotten the scholarship but I have the same credentials that you have.'"

Implied but not directly expressed in these comments is clearly the factor of race. Although race has played a part in students' being considered for the program, the students became focused on proving that academic ability, not race, was the primary reason they were selected. Another student's comments reflect this desire to prove their worth: "I was going to show everybody that I deserved the scholarship because there were some white people on the floor who were like, 'We don't even get this; we have higher SAT scores.' I was like so, I can do the work. I just wanted to show everybody I could do the work. I did pretty well those first two semesters and everything. I had hopes of seeing everyone else do well too, because it shows everybody that we can do well, you know."

Similarly another student stated, "I am certain I won't ever feel like we shouldn't have to prove ourselves so hard, but at the same time that's there, that's part of the responsibility of students in this type of program, which says, 'Look, we're just as talented as any other group out there.' And when you hear about things that happen to other students as far as the racial things that have occurred, it sort of makes you feel like, well, I'm going to do this, I'm going to show these people."

Beyond financial rewards, one reason for confrontations by white peers, and in some cases black peers, was the scholarship program's high public profile—the Meyerhoffs received significant attention from high-level administrators on the campus. Membership in a "select" group with a high profile automatically brought more intense scrutiny—as did the initial program mission to serve black students. Learning how to manage the perceptions that others have of you in a way that allows you to grow and move forward can be a challenge. Fortunately, the Meyerhoff students have the strong support of their families and the Meyerhoff group. However, even with several layers of support, these students still express a sense of responsibility to prove they are worthy.

Identifying with a Community of Peers

Although academic ability is a major factor in how high-ability black students come to understand who they are, connections with other students of color are also very important. Finding these connections can be a challenge. Many of the students gave examples of not having many black friends who were doing what they were doing in high school; consequently, their sense of a community of black scholars was undermined by the perception that blacks did not generally demonstrate an interest in academics. One student, reflecting on his high school experience, said:

> In high school, I was one of only two black students in the TAG [talented and gifted] classes. It was hard for me to get to know people and stuff in high school because I was studying and everything and it took a great deal of time. I was on the debate team. When I look back at things, [I realize] I was the only black person doing this, but at the time it didn't seem like that, you know. Getting to college and everything was like—man, I wonder if everyone had to go through the same thing I did. And not everyone did. [At college] there were a great deal of people who hadn't been the only black students, like at [my high school], a lot of people could ask each other questions and they were tight. . . . But in my situation, I was kind of isolated in a way, and when I got to UMBC, it [having black peers] did help me with the other people that lived there.

This student realized that other black students had different experiences in high school that included friendships and interactions with other high-achieving blacks. He admired people who could ask each other questions and who were "tight" because they were able to benefit from interacting within a community of "like-type" peers. For many high-ability black students, having close relationships with a group of peers would be a dream come true. Another student commented, "I don't want to make home sound like it was this really awful place to be, but when I was in high school, a lot of African American students didn't have the stamina or reports of doing well. Or their definition of doing well was getting by with 2.0, 2.5. And a 2.5 has never been good enough for me."

For many students, peer connections and networks change over time. Because high-ability blacks are often in classrooms with whites, they often have both academic and social relationships with white students. However, over time, black students may feel that their social needs cannot be completely met by a predominantly white social group. An example of how their needs change is reflected in this comment:

> I have two groups of friends: I have a group of friends that I met back in high school, and back in high school we did our little high school thing. They're mostly white, and like I said, all the times I was hanging out with them was cool, like a high school atmosphere. But when you go beyond that, you don't feel a part as much. Up at UMBC . . . , all my friends are black except the guys I just met. Everyone from UMBC, of course, they're all Meyerhoffs, so everyone is black. I can always hang out with them no matter what. I can go to a dance club or something and not feel out of place, and for me, it's kind of different from high school.

For most of the students I interviewed, making connections with other Meyerhoffs in college marked the first time they had found a group that reflected both their academic pursuits and their racial identity. These relationships provided the support they needed to be both black and intellectual. The students express a sense of comfort and even relief when talking about the relationships they had with the Meyerhoffs. Some students candidly admitted that they had made their decision to attend the university specifically because of the access it would give them to other high-achieving blacks—further evidence of their need to connect with a community of peers:

> I came to UMBC because of the program. Without the program, I would not be here. I'm from Silver Spring; if you think of going to a state school, you go to UMCP [University of Maryland, College Park]. I'm not accustomed to being in the Meyerhoff program with all high-achieving black students. I come from a predominantly white school, predominantly white neighborhoods, and I guess I have always been in predominantly white schools. The biggest thing I guess is just having other high-achieving black students.

For many of the students, coming to the Meyerhoff program was a welcome opportunity to express their interests in academics and still be embraced as authentically black in a community of peers who shared similar interests. Their comments about peers and their sense of self became much more positive as they reflected on their experiences with the Meyerhoffs. The important role of the community of Meyerhoffs is evident in the accounts of several students. One student explained:

> I think that it is very important that you interact a lot. Just the fact that there are other black students, that there's a concentration of us, and we are working together . . . that is very significant and impressive if you get into the Meyerhoff program. It's not just a scholarship given to a black student because [look] what happens with that type of scholarship at other schools: you may have a bunch of African American students with the scholarship so that they could pursue science degrees, but they are not put together like we are. They are not introduced to each other, they are not encouraged to become a family like we are. So therefore some of them may never get to know each other very well at other schools.

A deeper meaning is placed on the importance of the group as evidenced by the words "it is not just a scholarship" like other scholarships awarded to black students. This student emphasizes that the Meyerhoffs are "family," unlike other student groups and unlike the majority of these students' high school experiences. Another student expressed how this affected learning: "It is also a math- and science-related program, and typically blacks aren't expected to do as well, so [the program] forces us to get together and work together and do better in classes. The kids in the Meyerhoff program [have] pretty high [grades], and they're very competitive. That's another thing that would help and inspire people to do better, because you want to."

The support of the group was also seen as an empowering way to address issues in the classroom. For a student who might not ordinarily have talked with a faculty member, the Meyerhoff group provided extra support: "It [is] like having a whole bunch of people in your class and you can all get together and you can go to the teacher together and you can study together. It's just the togetherness that has been the most special thing to me. If I had been there alone, I probably would have done everything alone, but now with the program, I have a support group—that's what's special." In addition to providing academic support, the program offered opportunities for the students to engage in cultural activities that enhanced their sense of racial identity and cultural enrichment. One student explained, "The Meyerhoff program also gives you different cultural activities that you can go to. . . . things in theater and things for learning about what different black scholars have to say about the struggles of the race, things like that, that you can go to as well as just being around other black students who succeed and knowing that it's possible—of course, we know that it's possible."

Finally, several of the students I talked with expressed a desire to have a larger circle of friends or to connect with a broader group of peers beyond the Meyerhoffs. One student's own racial development influenced over time how she made decisions about her friends. She shared several reasons for her desire to have a more inclusive circle of peers:

> I study a lot with students from other ethnic backgrounds because it has been my experience that the black students are not quite as serious as some of the other students are, so I study with students of other cultural backgrounds. There was a time in my life when I was really, really a militant persona. I'm black, so it was black pride, fists in the air and fists coming out your hair and all that stuff. I didn't want to have a lot of friends of other ethnic backgrounds. I didn't see the importance of it, but now I do.

The Significance of Faculty

Faculty play a crucial role in helping high-achieving black students find the space to blend their academic interests with other concerns including issues pertaining to race. Research indicates that it can be difficult for black students to establish meaningful relationships with white faculty (Allen, 1992; Fleming, 1984). Part of the success of the Meyerhoffs is hidden in the details of the program. There is a concerted effort to structure contact with faculty and to ensure that faculty are informed of the students' caliber. These efforts enhance positive interactions with faculty. Faculty-student contact, both formal and informal, is one of the most important factors in students' academic success (Pascarella and Terenzini, 1991). One of the female students I interviewed described how beneficial her interactions were both personally and academically. Her comments reflect the fact that she was able to find support for her academic self and other parts of her identity including race and, in this case, gender:

> There is one professor here that I am especially close to. I took an internship with her in the biology department, and it's really turned out to be a great relationship. I respect her as a person, and she is a wonderful, modern-thinking woman and we talk. . . . She's a white professor, but she can talk freely with me about problems with being a minority in science and being a woman, things like that. We talk about fun things. I've developed a good relationship with her, and the Meyerhoff faculty, . . . and they've given me a lot of emotional support.

The ability to talk freely was clearly what impressed this student and allowed her to feel comfortable in establishing a relationship with the faculty member. Similarly, another student stated, "I have one professor that taught me last summer, and I am now doing research with her. I'm taking it for credit, but it's not really a class, we're more friends than professor and student. We can talk. It's not one of those relationships where she is talking down to me or questioning if I'm smart enough. But we can talk about things that are going on in the research project."

The most compelling part of this student's comment is the notion that a faculty member is not questioning if she is smart enough but rather is interacting with the student comfortably and assuming that she is capable. When faculty members assume that students are capable and have something to contribute, they help eliminate some of the barriers that minority students often encounter in the academy. The more a faculty member is able to establish a relationship based on mutual respect and not out of obligation, the greater the likelihood the student will consider the faculty member's interest as genuine and sincere. One student captured this well, saying:

> I worked with her during the summer and during the fall semester. I haven't had a class with her yet—I may have one with her next semester—but I go to her if I have trouble with classes or just to talk about things. I go to her . . . because it means a lot to me because it's not like she's my adviser or I'm in her class and she's getting something out of this; she's doing this for my benefit. So her interest means a lot to me, and I drop by the lab now and then just to say hi to her and get her input into situations.

Promoting Learning via Identity Development

Faculty can be instrumental in helping black students blend their racial and intellectual identities by creating conditions in and outside of the classroom that reinforce and support the development of a strong sense of self. First, faculty must cultivate opportunities for classroom dialogue, for several reasons. Faculty will have an opportunity to learn about students' development, including their racial identity development, by observing and listening to what students say. As faculty observe students interacting, they will be able to evaluate the degree of students' comfort talking about a wide range of topics within peer groups. When appropriate and possible, faculty should open discussions pertaining to race, racism, and other forms of oppression. These opportunities in the classroom will give all students (especially high-ability black students) a chance to think out loud with peers and faculty about a very complex topic.

Students also learn how to construct conversations across race and expand their understanding as they hear the thoughts and ideas of others. For some high-ability students, incorporating discussions on race in the classroom may provide an opportunity for them to discuss some of their own difficulties in "fitting in" with the extended black community and the majority community.

Second, faculty should create a supportive community for learning. For high-ability students, finding a supportive "like-type" community is especially valuable. Even if we are unable to provide a racial "like-type" community, we can apply the factors that make these communities successful in our classrooms. Faculty should create more opportunities for students to work in groups. There are tremendous benefits to group work. However, it is important when assigning groups to consider having more than one minority member per group. Too often minority students are spread so thinly among groups that they become "token" representatives within each group. Though there may be some advantages of having different "perspectives" in each group, the disadvantage for minority group members is that they have fewer interactions on projects with students who share racial affiliation and intellectual interests. When students work in groups, they may feel more comfortable asking the professor questions about an assignment and voicing an opinion different from the professor's. With the support of a group, some students may feel more empowered to share their perspective. Students' voices in this chapter show that high-ability black students benefit from having a critical mass of blacks to whom they can relate. If we create the support of a critical mass of peers, we may provide the support all students need to learn more and to be open to new ideas.

Third, faculty should use their interactions with students (formally and informally) to add to a student's sense of self rather than to subtract from it. Adding to a student's sense of self means that a faculty member understands what the student values and respects and affirms that for the student. Once you have affirmed what a student values, you can add to their learning by suggesting that they "also read" or "also consider" different viewpoints, instead of proffering discouraging or dismissive remarks such as "Don't bother with that; that won't serve you well here." Once we find ways to support students in their identity development, we open channels of trust that allow us to engage them more in the academic process and ultimately promote their learning.

To support students' development, we must be willing to learn more about racial identity development theories, including white racial identity theory. Understanding more about the racial identity literature will provide an alternative framework for faculty to understand behaviors and attitudes they may see in the classroom. We must challenge stereotypical assumptions we have about the academic interest and abilities of black students, increasing our awareness of our own development around issues of race and race relations. Even more important, we must engage in a level of risk-taking in the classroom to discuss a set of issues that many of us (personally or professionally) may feel uncomfortable confronting. If we are not careful, we can do more harm than good opening a dialogue on race or oppression. Nevertheless, it is important that we improve our strategies for enhancing all students' learning and in so doing experiment with new forms of pedagogy and new sources of power in the classroom. Students look for cues that we, too, struggle with, and we share some of their experiences. Consequently, if we learn to raise these issues comfortably, we can work with our students to create authentic experiences in the classroom that enhance development and learning for everyone.

References

Allen, W. R. "Correlates of Black Student Adjustment, Achievement, and Aspirations at a Predominantly White Southern University." In G. Thomas (ed.), *Black Students in Higher Education: Conditions and Experiences in the 1970s.* Westport, Conn.: Greenwood Press, 1981.

Allen, W. R. "The Color of Success: African-American College Student Outcomes at Predominantly White and Historically Black Public Colleges and Universities." *Harvard Educational Review,* 1992, *62,* 26–44.

Cooley, M. R., Cornell, D. G., and Lee, C. "Peer Acceptance and Self-Concept of Black Students in a Summer Gifted Program." *Journal for Education of the Gifted,* 1991, *14,* 166–177.

Cross, W. E. *Shades of Black: Diversity in African-American Identity.* Philadelphia: Temple University Press, 1991.

Fleming, J. *Blacks in College: A Comparative Study of Students' Success in Black and White Institutions.* San Francisco: Jossey-Bass, 1984.

Ford, D. Y. *Reversing Underachievement Among Gifted Black Students: Promising Practices and Programs.* Education and Psychology of the Gifted Series. New York: Teachers College Press, Columbia University, 1996.

Fordham, S., and Ogbu, J. "Black Students' School Success: Coping with the Burden of Acting White." *Urban Review,* 1986, *18,* 176–207.

Hrabowski, F. A., III, Maton, K. I., and Greif, G. L. *Beating the Odds: Raising Academically Successful African American Males.* New York: Oxford University Press, 1998.

Hurtado, S., and others. "Enacting Diverse Learning Environments: Improving the Climate for Racial/Ethnic Diversity in Higher Education." *ASHE-ERIC,* 1999, *26* (entire issue 8).

Lindstrom, R., and Van Sant, S. "Special Issues in Working with Gifted Minority Adolescents." *Journal of Counseling and Development,* 1986, *64,* 583–586.

Nettles, M., Theony, A., and Gosman, E. J. "Comparative and Predictive Analysis of Black and White Students' College Campus Achievement and Experiences." *Journal of Higher Education,* 1986, *57,* 289–317.

Olszewski-Kubilius, P. M., and Scott, J. M. "An Investigation of the College and Career Counseling Needs of Economically Disadvantaged Minority Gifted Students." *Roeper Review,* 1992, *14,* 141–148.

Pascarella, E. T., and Terenzini, P. T. *How College Affects Students: Findings and Insights from Twenty Years of Research.* San Francisco: Jossey-Bass, 1991.

Sedlacek, W. E. "Black Students on White Campuses: 20 Years of Research." *Journal of College Student Personnel,* 1987, *28,* 484–495.

Serwatka, T. S., Deering, S., and Stoddard, A. "Correlates of the Underrepresentation of Black Students in Classes for Gifted Students." *Journal of Negro Education,* 1989, *58,* 520–530.

SHARON FRIES-BRITT is an assistant professor in the Department of Education Policy, Planning, and Administration at the University of Maryland, College Park.

Cultural identity development is linked to critical thinking and intercultural competence. This chapter articulates those connections and describes strategies for dealing with difference effectively in the classroom.

Expressing Cultural Identity in the Learning Community: Opportunities and Challenges

Anna M. Ortiz

One of the most persistent and problematic dilemmas I have experienced as a university faculty member is teaching and dealing with difference in the classroom. There are moments when I feel pride and success with the challenges my students embrace and conquer with grace and intelligence, but those times are far outweighed by moments of silence, misunderstanding, and anger. When a faculty member "allows" cultural identity and its associated issues to take center stage in the classroom, the outcome is always tenable. Because of the risk inherent in addressing and promoting cultural identity, many faculty members choose not to "go there." Excluding these different perspectives produces outcomes that are more troublesome than those that arise through taking the risk. Inhibiting the expression of cultural identity in the classroom denies learning opportunities that not only promote the development of complex meaning-making but also strengthens students' sense of self and furthers the acquisition of the types of competence needed to thrive in a diverse world community. In this chapter, I address some of the common areas of difficulty when infusing cultural identity in learning communities by sharing the insights I have gained through both research and classroom teaching.

I begin by sharing the development of my own perspectives about cultural identity. Anyone who chooses to step in front of a classroom and actively pursue these topics needs to engage in an examination of his or her own cultural identity. It cannot be subject matter that stands removed from the self. Faculty members who neglect this self-exploration run the risk of responding with defensiveness and falling into the all too familiar role of the unchallengeable authority. My own story will serve as an example, as it reveals the complexity of issues surrounding cultural identity in the learning community. It highlights the individual differences found in culturally different students; the contradictions of multiple ethnic heritages; the intersection of gender, class, and ethnicity; and the pedagogy in the academy that often inhibits us from seeing students as holding knowledge that may better inform our own.

I grew up with a very strong sense of being Mexican American. I also knew that my mother's family was not Mexican, as I was constantly reminded that that was the real reason I did not speak Spanish. What I did not realize is that I was half white; in fact, I'm still processing that. My mother is Portuguese, as was my *madrina* (godmother), whom I grew up very close to. There were so many congruities between the Portuguese and Mexican cultures that it felt seamless. Because both sides of my family are filled with very strong women, I also developed a very strong identity as a woman and a feminist. I lack memories of experiences as racist or discriminatory, although I can now reflect on the fact that I was the only Mexican American student in the college-prep courses at my high school, despite the large number of Mexican families and their children in the community, as evidence of discrimination. In contrast, college offered me many insights. There, I was a "racial" being. At times I was not "Mexican" enough; at other times I was a representative of Mexican American students without even knowing it.

My professional experiences as a student affairs administrator and later as a teacher in the college setting taught me about the experiences of culturally different students in the academy. Working with Latino/a students in a residential cultural house taught me a great deal about issues of policy and identity politics in the university but even more about the struggles and successes of very special and unique students. My comfortable middle-class upbringing and the guidance and pressure of my college-educated father and his high goals for me supported my college pursuits. Working with those students in Casa Cautehmoc, who straddled two worlds—the home and academy—gave me insights that would have otherwise taken me years to develop.

These experiences led me to think about ethnic identity and cultural identity as a foundation for my research agenda in studying college students. Even in research, the students who have been participants in my studies have taught me far more than the hours I spent "reviewing the literature." Three studies in particular inform what I know about cultural identity in the learning community. The first was my study on ethnic identity in college students (Ortiz, 1997). The findings told me that students who live and grow up in very diverse environments may develop and experience their ethnic identity in ways that were quite different from the models I found in the literature. The second is a study of a cross-cultural mediation program at a major university (Ortiz, 1995). In this study, I followed a diverse group of women through a course on conflict and diversity and their training to become cross-cultural mediators. Intensely studying a "multicultural education" program helped me understand that the development of what I called racial understanding progresses through a cognitive development process. The third is a recent study on the development of intercultural competence in U.S. students studying abroad (Moore and Ortiz, 1999). In this study, the literature review did introduce me to many new ideas such as intercultural perspective taking and intercultural competence. The students in the study helped me see that the development of intercultural competence depends on risk taking, considering other worldviews, and deconstructing and then reconstructing one's identity.

Teaching college students has shown me that there are a wealth of opportunities to enhance epistemological development through the exploration of various manifestations of cultural identity in the learning community. Throughout the remainder of the chapter, I discuss this assumption within the framework of intercultural competence described by Sorti (1990). Within his framework, intrapersonal, interpersonal, and cognitive dimensions merge to create an interculturally competent person. The development of cultural identity, worldview, and intercultural perspective taking is related to these dimensions. Cultural identity is primarily an intrapersonal, psychological task but is enhanced by interaction with others. Worldview is primarily a cognitive phenomenon but is also reflective of the development of the self, an intrapersonal construct. Intercultural perspective taking blends all three dimensions. The ability to take the perspective of another is a cognitive skill that is also interpersonal in that it enhances interactions, but it is also intrapersonal because it requires the development of empathy. Vibrant classroom settings have the potential to attend to the interpersonal, intrapersonal, and cognitive dimensions in unique ways.

The Development of Cultural Identity

The terms *ethnic identity, racial identity,* and *cultural identity* are used interchangeably, depending on the focus of the model being described. Ethnic identity as a construct has two aspects: content and salience. The content of ethnic identity refers to the customs, language, behaviors, music, literature, heroes, values, and worldview that a group with a common ethnic heritage shares. The salience of ethnic identity describes the degree to which membership in the group and the content of ethnic identity are important to the individual's sense of self.

Racial identity development models include both the content and salience of an ethnic identity but add the process by which individuals come to terms with the consequences of that group's place in society. Realizing that racism exists and developing a positive self-concept as a member of a racial group are emphasized in these models.

I use *cultural identity* in this chapter because it is a broader term that encompasses racial, ethnic, and cultural groups. Cultural identity is very similar to ethnic and racial identity, but the commonality does not have to be ethnic. Groups with common values, customs, practices, and experiences might be religious groups or gay, lesbian, or bisexual communities. Members of cultural groups, ethnic or otherwise, experience varying degrees of identification with the group, participate in the customs or activities of the group, and have similar belief systems. They also often experience oppression in ways similar to those described by racial identity models. Many authors (Atkinson, Morten, and Sue, 1993; Cross, 1991; Helms, 1995; Phinney, 1992) posit that the degree of identification an individual may have with a culture is a developmental process of exploration and commitment to that group.

Enculturation and acculturation are processes that also describe the development of cultural identity, although not necessarily through stage models. Enculturation is the socialization process by which individuals acquire the host of cultural and psychological qualities that are necessary to function as a member of one's group. Acculturation is the product of culture learning that occurs as a result of contact between the members of two or more culturally distinct groups, a process of attitudinal and behavioral change undergone, willingly or unwillingly, by individuals who reside in multicultural societies (Casas and Pytluk, 1995). Native Americans, Asian Americans, and Latino/as exemplify the problematic nature of acculturation and group diversity. There is great diversity within these groups. Native Americans are members of distinct tribes, but many members also have mixed ethnic heritages. Asian American and Hispanics come from a wide range of countries and also differ within and between specific national groups by generational status (time in the United States). The enculturation and acculturation processes explain how people come to feel a part of their specific cultural group while embracing the larger culture. Choney, Berryhill-Paapke, and Robbins (1995) propose an acculturation model that determines the degree to which a person has experienced acculturation to mainstream culture. They call the levels of acculturation traditional, transitional, bicultural, assimilated, and marginal (unconnected to either culture). Acculturation to mainstream culture may occur along cognitive (language and customs), behavioral (activities), affective or spiritual (connection to others and religion), and social or environmental (place they live, who they socialize with) dimensions. For example, a traditional Japanese American may keep the language and customs learned in Japan, participate in traditional Japanese activities, practice Buddhism, and live in a Japanese enclave in a large city.

Opportunities for Learning. Students from distinct ethnic or cultural groups often experience both enculturation and acculturation in their new environment. The earlier example of the woman who gained a greater sense of academic self-confidence once she began to learn more about the history of African Americans also serves as an example of someone who is becoming more enculturated to her own cultural group. Likewise, many college students who come from highly enculturated families and communities experience acculturation when they come to college. A Korean student talks about his own acculturation:

Although there might be some negative aspects to the mainstream, there are a lot of positive points which Asian cultures lack, like being independent, being open-minded. I think those are all a part of mainstream America and how the Western culture really acts. I did adapt a lot. I think the phrase "Korean American" is appropriate because you do have both cultures, and if you can't adapt or if you can't accept the two cultures, then I think the term "Korean American" is misleading.

This student also demonstrates how students consider new possibilities that may be seen as positive contributions to their personality and sense of self. His experience in evaluating parental values and integrating newly discovered values into his sense of self illustrates further connections to moral and epistemic development.

Cross's Model of Nigrescence (1991), which Mary Howard-Hamilton discussed in Chapter Five, is one of the earliest and most studied models of cultural identity (although it is a racial identity development model). The starting point of the model is marked low salience of race, and the endpoint is an integrated personality where a positive sense of self includes commitment to being black and to the progress of the racial group and improvement of conditions for members of that group. The process is one where the development of Nigrescence is a resocializing experience. In terms of the learning community or a classroom environment, there are many opportunities and challenges in this framework alone.

Students who are in the encounter and immersion-emersion stages provide excellent examples of how exploration in the classroom can assist in the development of "self." The resocializing and reeducation process that begins in encounter may often occur as a result of course reading, lectures, and discussion, especially if the student is in an ethnic studies course. One of the students from my study on ethnic identity tells of the importance such curricula had in her encounter-stage experience:

> I was never taught true history. All I was ever taught was that black people were brought over here as slaves and it was a good thing that happened because we weren't very civilized. Once I came to college, I became interested in African American history and African history. It really change me. I changed everything about my life because then I was proud of my identity. I'm proud to be black, proud to be African. I didn't realize the transformation at first, but as I looked back and saw how my thinking started to change as soon as I started taking those classes, I realized I probably would have done better in school. Maybe I would have had a 4.0 and gotten a scholarship to a better school.

This student not only developed a positive sense of self but also had the insight to connect how a lack of attention to the history of her cultural group inhibited her success as a student. The *liberation* she experienced by integrating alternative perspectives to her view of the world allowed her to change her thinking in ways that had profound effects for her, personally and academically.

The opportunity for peer learning also presents itself in contexts where students are encouraged to talk about the development of their cultural identity. Students who exhibit the extroverted enthusiasm of the immersion-emersion stage may serve as role models for other students. A Latina from the same study tells of what she learned from a peer who was in the immersion-emersion stage: "My friend is always saying 'I'm proud to be black.' She always says, 'Stand up for yourself!' She never lets anybody get her down or anything. She's always very positive about being black. Well, I'm proud to be Mexican! That's one thing I learned from her." Students' responses to their immersion-emersion peers often reflect their own epistemic development. The quote shows a relationship to knowledge that is more authority-driven: the speaker models the "more developed" student.

Another student offers a glimpse of how she is beginning to think contextually about her own cultural identity, reflecting interpersonal, intrapersonal, and cognitive domains:

> There's a big issue about "are you Chicana, Latina, Mexican American, or what?" And I identify more with Mexican American. I don't know, I guess that's because I have been told that since I was young, . . . but I see myself more as a Mexican American, and that's my heritage. . . . To be Chicana, I think, is more political. I think that is a political term. . . . I know about different issues that they advocate, but I don't participate, so I don't feel comfortable calling myself Chicana. . . . But there have been times that I have said that I am something else, because of the environment. . . . [I was at] a conference and . . . everybody else called themselves Chicana and so did I. But I have to say that I can't identify myself as one.

There is the distinct sense that this student is in the midst of the encounter stage. Though confused about how to identify herself, she shows quite clearly that she is beginning to make meaning of her world and herself in different ways. She is beginning to grasp the notion that knowledge, even what she knows about herself, is often grounded in context. Simply discussing the various labels students use to describe themselves can elicit complex reasoning that helps students think critically about dimensions of the self.

Challenges Surrounding the Expression of Cultural Identity. There is also a sense that the student is grappling with how to interact with her more politically oriented peers, which is demonstrative of one of the more difficult challenges of having students with differing developmental experiences with cultural identity in the same classroom. Students in the immersion-emersion stage often show little acknowledgment of contextual differences in cultural identity development. Students whose views differ may feel that they are not a "good enough" cultural or ethnic person and may be inhibited to continue exploration of this part of the self. This may be an especially vexing problem for mixed-race students or for students who may be in the pre-encounter and encounter stages. This is also a problem for students who strive to balance competing cultural identities. How does gender or sexual orientation intersect with this process? Does being gay or lesbian take precedence over being black? Does one cultural identity have to take precedence over another? These are all important questions as we develop positive learning environments for students.

The work of Helms (1995) and Tatum (1992) demonstrates the challenge of negotiating difference in the classroom setting when students are from different ethnic backgrounds and at different levels of development. The resistance of white students and some students of color to discussing these issues in ways that reinforce complex meaning-making cannot be overstated. The professor must dance along the fine line between engagement and alienation in these matters! I borrow from the tenets of cultural identity models, perspective taking, and worldview when designing lectures and class activities intended to lessen initial tension about the subject and then work systematically toward more complex understandings of culture and its relationships to self and society (Ortiz and Rhoads, 1999).

Cultural identity models also present a challenge for us in our own learning. Stage models comfort us because they appear to offer some level of certainty, but we always have to be aware of the diversity among individuals in any group of people organized around any variable. Another error we make when learning about cultural identity models as they apply to students is that we too often try to predict human and student behavior instead of trying to understand it. I find that students react rather strongly to stage models. They can tell immediately when the models do not reflect their own experiences or those of people they know. So presenting models in ways that tell students what their experiences were, are, or are likely to be may actually diminish our credibility with them. It is more productive to proceed with caution and to recognize that models can only explain how certain individuals *may* be at different points in time.

Culture and Worldview

There is a direct connection between cultural identity and worldview. Our culture defines how we view the world around us because it shapes our values, determines our interactions with the dominant culture, and directs our attention by telling us what is important in the world we inhabit. As a consequence of our culture, we pay more attention to some things than to others. Worldview is our abstract understandings of the world, involving broad domains of life such as human nature, interpersonal relationships, physical nature, time, and activities (Trevino, 1996). It is formed by culture—both the culture one shares with one's group and the culture that evolves from one's unique experiences. Culture informs our interpretation of the events around us and shapes our understanding of the people we come in contact with. The connection is so close and direct that we are seldom conscious that this influence is at work.

In a learning community where there are different cultures, clashes arise when differing worldviews prevent people from understanding what is important or valued by other communities and individuals within the university. For example, if my worldview is the dominant one, there are certain values and understandings of the world I possess—for example, I may not understand what miseducation means, or I may not understand why people need to express their culture through activities, organizations, and courses. I may not understand why some teaching methods privilege some while inhibiting others. I may believe that the world and knowledge are logical, orderly, and fair.

However, if I'm a culturally different person, my worldview may be completely different, and that changes not only the way I view others and society but also my entire relationship with knowledge. For example, there are some things I "know" from my experience as a culturally different person:

- People may not succeed even if they try very hard; meritocracy is therefore a false concept.
- Our legal system does not always operate in a fair and equitable way; thus justice does not exist for all people.
- In making life choices, I have to consider the needs of others, the expectations of those I respect, and the progress of my community; so rugged individualism, where the needs of the individual override the needs of the group, is not an option for me.

Meritocracy, justice, and individualism are deeply ingrained in American culture. Yet many of our students know that these "givens" are not a part of their realities. As a result, they come to know that knowledge and truth are contextual, that authorities do not know all the answers, and that their life experiences very much determine their realities. This may be why my study on the cognitive dimensions of racial understanding showed that women of color came to know at higher stages of cognitive development. The models advanced by Perry (1970), Baxter Magolda (1992), and King and Kitchener (1994) all posit that lower stages of cognitive development involve concrete thinking and a belief in absolute knowledge, whereas higher levels reflect an ability to consider knowledge based on context, using judgment derived from personal experiences and evidence from other sources and from the perspective of others. This raises the distinct possibility that culturally different worldviews may lead to greater complexity in thinking, as suggested by King and Shuford (1996).

Using this often untapped potential in the learning community can increase critical thinking for all students. Students who construct their own knowledge based on their worldview and experiences help others challenge authority—either the authority of the instructor or the authority inherent in the printed word. When the classroom climate invites critique rather than suppress it, all students benefit. Those with differing worldviews feel that their knowledge has a place in the academy, and other students both learn from these views and begin to understand that they can develop and project their own voice in the discourse. The idea that knowledge is not static but contextual is fundamental to the development of critical thinking.

Intercultural Perspective Taking and Intercultural Competence

As we learn more about our own worldview and the worldview of others, we develop the ability to take the intercultural perspective of others. Intercultural perspective taking (Kappler, 1998; Steglitz, 1993) is a cognitive skill that enables the individual to recognize the existence and impact of culture and understand the ways in which cultures can vary. In various studies, the ability to generate possible cultural explanations as a cause of problems in intercultural interactions—the cognitive dimension—accounts for up to 80 percent of the variance in intercultural competence. The cognitive nature of intercultural perspective taking is highlighted by Steglitz's model of how we come to understand how behavior and perspectives are shaped by culture, how culture influences individuals, how culturally different people may be influenced by their culture (or cultures), and how culture might influence the interpretation and perception of a situation.

In my research with students studying abroad (Moore and Ortiz, 1999), intercultural perspective taking included an ability not only to take the perspective of a culturally different other but also to examine one's own culture from the perspective of people outside it. Students were forced to confront realities of life in America and how the world feels about Americans. One student said, "I never realized how American I was until I lived in Italy. . . . You realize exactly who you are and what you represent." This put them in the "third position," forced to stand outside their identity as Americans and outside the culture they were living in. Thinking about being an American while in a foreign country caused students to evaluate and eventually to value both the host culture and American culture. They saw the foreign and environmental policies of the American government in a different light. They were able to identify the isolationist attitude of Americans with regard to the rest of the world. Some time after developing a sense of shame about being American, students began to evaluate the host culture in a more objective way. They came to the conclusion that cultures and societies cannot be evaluated along the simplistic lines of right and wrong. They saw that aspects of society could be valuable in some cases and damaging in others. This became a much more realistic and comfortable position for students to inhabit. The ability to take the third position, outside both cultures, allowed them to take perspective in entirely new ways that led to more complex cognitive reasoning and a more complex and nuanced worldview.

The ability to take the perspective of culturally different persons leads to the development of intercultural competence. Intercultural competence depends on the development of three separate but related dimensions: cognitive (knowledge and cognition), intrapersonal (identity, self-education), and interpersonal (Sorti, 1990). In the study of intercultural competence in American students abroad (Moore and Ortiz, 1999), we identified the characteristics of the interculturally competent person. Interculturally competent students are critical thinkers (embodying one of the primary goals of higher education). They suspend judgment until all the evidence is in. They include a diverse range of knowledge in what they consider to be evidence. They have enough self-knowledge (and a requisite positive sense of self) to know their own limits and can take positive steps to alleviate difficult situations. The process of examining situations from different perspectives encourages a cognitive flexibility that leads to better problem solving both in and out of the classroom.

Classroom Strategies to Develop Intercultural Competence

How are classroom communities where this type of interaction takes place developed? First, it is imperative that students begin talking in class as engaged participants in discussion and with other class members. Developing a sense of community in the classroom encourages students to take risks in sharing their own knowledge and in questioning students and professors about what they know. Interactive acquaintance activities conducted during the first class session can begin this process. I like to offer activities where students get to know personal things about each other and then move the discussion to how they can use this new learning community to support their learning and development. I encourage the sharing of individual cultural characteristics among students to supplement the traditional "name, rank, and major" that usually accompanies such introductions. I might ask students to share three things about themselves that cannot be known from simply observing their appearance. After initial activities, I might then ask students to share what they consider to be their cultural heritage and values. There are many benefits to beginning courses with these types of activities. Students begin to learn about cultural identity from one another, which reinforces the acceptance of all students in the classroom. They start to learn about the impact of each individual's worldview on knowledge and experiences. The following student tells what she has learned from other students in one of her racially diverse classes:

> Interacting with them has helped because most of them know more about their cultural background and traditions. They made me want to go and ask questions about my cultural background, because they are always sharing with me and I'm really a little ignorant. I've never really been taught. So I have

to go to the library and check it out or ask aunts and uncles or Mom and Dad. So it's helped me because when I was hanging around in high school with [members of] just my own culture, we never asked these questions—the curiosity was never there.

Second, using cooperative, collaborative, or active learning methods, such as the formation of base groups, can also be helpful in the process of community building. Participating in interactive discussions, case study analyses (similar to critical incidents), and small group activities allows students to begin trusting their own meaning-making and also helps them contextualize course content so that it is reflective of their experiences. If students are able to discover the key concepts I wish to cover for the day on their own through discussion or questioning one another, they retain those concepts much better than if I delivered them from the lectern. I also learn about other cultures and the impact of the college environment on culturally diverse students by listening to the way in which they come to reason about key concepts. There may be disciplines where this type of learning and teaching is more difficult, but there are probably points of difference or controversy in almost any content that students can explore in ways that allow divergent opinions and critical thinking to emerge. These pedagogical techniques help students trust that personal perspectives are welcomed in the class and understand that voicing contextual interpretations of material is acceptable in this classroom.

Third, it is important to design assignments that are also reflective of engaged pedagogy. In writing assignments, students in my courses need to combine their own perspectives and experiences with those of the course material. This higher-order task asks students to engage with the material in more critical ways than simply recounting the story line. When students attempt these assignments for the first time, they almost always have a difficult time. Their previous educational experiences have taught them that there are two kinds of written work, the traditional research paper and the reflective journal. Combining elements of the two requires critical analysis and the inclusion of knowledge drawn from personal contexts. Assignments like this call for the inclusion of worldview and make perspective taking almost natural. I also use group projects frequently. These assignments prompt students to include diverse perspectives in the finished product and help students develop communication and mediation skills in creating the product. The time they spend in contact with students who may not necessarily be a part of their social group also aids in learning more about students from different backgrounds. Intentionally grouping students is also helpful in meeting this goal. Of course, any professor who has attempted projects like this knows that they are fraught with challenges, but I believe they are ones worth facing up to.

In conclusion, the true challenges lie in helping students discover the value in learning about culture and its impact on individuals, interpersonal interactions, and society. The bigger challenge is generating excitement about these discoveries. This means being patient with students and ourselves: we need to understand that learning is also a developmental journey. This is perhaps the biggest challenge—to remain patient yet push for change. Mistakes will be made, both by students and professors. In fact, an unexpected outcome may be that students learn that even people with doctorates make mistakes, and that serves to heighten their confidence as constructors of knowledge. Creating communities where cultural identity can be expressed openly and applied to knowledge learned also means creating communities where students feel safe in taking risks, which fosters a hunger for analysis and reflection of content regardless of its disciplinary origins. And that is an honorable goal for any educator.

References

Atkinson, D. R., Morten, G., and Sue, D. W. *Counseling American Minorities: A Cross-Cultural Perspective.* (4th ed.) Dubuque, Iowa: Brown and Benchmark, 1993.

Baxter Magolda, M. B. *Knowing and Reasoning in College: Gender-Related Patterns in Students' Intellectual Development.* San Francisco: Jossey-Bass, 1992.

Casas, J. M., and Pytluk, S. D. "Hispanic Identity Development: Implications for Research and Practice." In J. G. Ponterotto, J. M. Casas, L. A. Suzuki, and C. M. Alexander (eds.), *Handbook of Multicultural Counseling.* Thousand Oaks, Calif.: Sage, 1995.

Choney, S. K., Berryhill-Paapke, E., and Robbins, R. R. "The Acculturation of American Indians: Developing Frameworks for Research and Practice." In J. G. Ponterotto, J. M. Casas, L. A. Suzuki, and C. M. Alexander (eds.), *Handbook of Multicultural Counseling.* Thousand Oaks, Calif.: Sage, 1995.

Cross, W. E. J. *Shades of Black: Diversity in African-American Identities.* Philadelphia: Temple University Press, 1991.

Helms, J. E. "An Update of Helms' White and People of Color Racial Identity Models." In J. G. Ponterotto, J. M. Casas, L. A. Suzuki, and C. M. Alexander (eds.), *Handbook of Multicultural Counseling.* Thousand Oaks, Calif.: Sage, 1995.

Kappler, B. J. "Refining Intercultural Perspective-Taking." Unpublished doctoral dissertation, University of Minnesota, 1998.

King, P. M., and Kitchener, K. S. *Developing Reflective Judgment: Understanding and Promoting Intellectual Growth and Critical Thinking in Adolescents and Adults.* San Francisco: Jossey-Bass, 1994.

King, P. M., and Shuford, B. C. "A Multicultural View Is a More Cognitively Complex View: Cognitive Development and Multicultural Education." *American Behavioral Scientist,* 1996, *40,* 153–164.

Moore, K, A., and Ortiz, A. M. "The Intercultural Competence Project: Site Visit and Focus Group Report." Report to the Institute on the International Education of Students, Michigan State University, 1999.

Ortiz, A. M. "Promoting Racial Understanding: A Study of Educational and Developmental Interventions." Paper presented at the annual meeting of the Association for the Study of Higher Education, Orlando, Fla., Nov. 1995.

Ortiz, A. M. "Defining Oneself in a Multicultural World: Ethnic Identity in College Students." Unpublished doctoral dissertation, University of California, Los Angeles, 1997.

Ortiz, A. M., and Rhoads, R. A. "Deconstructing Whiteness as Part of a Multicultural Educational Framework: From Theory to Practice." *Journal of College Student Development,* 2000, *41,* 81–91.

Perry, W. G., Jr. *Forms of Intellectual and Ethical Development in the College Years: A Scheme.* Austin, Tex.: Holt, Rinehart and Winston, 1970.

Phinney, J. S. "The Multigroup Ethnic Identity Measure: A New Scale for Use with Diverse Groups." *Journal of Adolescent Research,* 1992, *7,* 156–176.

Sorti, C. *The Art of Crossing Cultures.* Yarmouth, Maine: Intercultural Press, 1990.

Steglitz, I. "Intercultural Perspective-Taking: The Impact of Study Abroad." Unpublished doctoral dissertation, University of Minnesota, Minneapolis, 1993.

Tatum, B. "Talking About Race, Learning About Racism: The Application of Racial Identity Development Theory in the Classroom." *Harvard Educational Review,* 1992, *62,* 1–24.

Trevino, J. G. "Worldview and Change in Cross-Cultural Counseling." *Counseling Psychologist,* 1996, *24,* 198–215.

ANNA M. ORTIZ is an assistant professor in the Department of Educational Administration at Michigan State University, East Lansing.

8

Gay, lesbian, and bisexual students often first acknowledge their sexual orientation and explore their identities in college. Faculty can play an active role in creating a welcoming and inclusive learning environment for these students.

Creating a Positive Learning Environment for Gay, Lesbian, and Bisexual Students

Nancy J. Evans

"What does sexual orientation have to do with learning in the classroom?" "Won't acknowledging issues related to sexual orientation just cause unnecessary controversy in the classroom?" "My field is chemistry; what does that have to do with sexual orientation?"

Such questions are very common when faculty are asked to consider the learning needs of gay, lesbian, and bisexual students. I address these topics in this chapter, first by listening to the voices of students talking about their experiences with supportive faculty. Then I present a model of how individuals develop a gay, lesbian, or bisexual identity. I next examine how experiences in the classroom affect this process. I conclude by returning to the questions I initially posed.

Students' Experiences of Faculty Support

How do faculty make a difference in the lives of gay, lesbian, and bisexual students? In 1998, Iowa State University established the Safe Zone program to increase visible support for gay, lesbian, and bisexual individuals on campus. Faculty and staff who wished to indicate they were supportive of gay, lesbian, and bisexual individuals requested and displayed a Safe Zone sticker on their office doors. This sticker consisted of the words *Safe Zone* printed below a pink triangle (a symbol commonly associated with the lesbian, gay, and bisexual communities). Following are statements made by two students concerning what it meant to them to see Safe Zone stickers on the doors of their faculty (Evans, 1998):

NEW DIRECTIONS FOR TEACHING AND LEARNING, no. 82, Summer 2000   © Jossey-Bass Publishers

It meant a lot to me about what kind of questions and what kind of interpretations I'm allowed to share in the classroom. If I've seen a professor's office and it has a sticker, that controls the amount of risks that I'm willing [to take] in my papers and in my class discussions. It allows me to make an assumption that this is an ally.

I came out to my parents at the end of January and that was a very [stressful] two weeks. And I knew which professors I could talk [to] about getting an extension on a paper because I was up dealing with family stuff all night. I knew when this would be OK to bring up. . . . It made it possible to come out to my parents and still continue on with life because I didn't want to drop this semester; I just needed a couple of weeks of flexibility and I got it.

Research suggests that learning is affected by motivational factors intrinsic to the individual, such as self-confidence, perceived importance of learning, and expectations for success (McMillan and Forsyth, 1991), as well as the social context, including whether or not the learning environment is encouraging and supportive (Tiberius and Billson, 1991). Learning is enhanced when students feel validated (Rendón, 1994) and when they experience positive interactions with peers and faculty both in and outside of the classroom (Kuh, Douglas, Lund, and Ramin-Gyurnek, 1994). Because of the hostility that gay, lesbian, and bisexual students regularly experience, these students often question themselves and approach any situation with caution. To ensure that lesbian, gay, and bisexual students are afforded opportunities to learn equivalent to those of other students, faculty must take an active role in creating a supportive climate. Understanding factors involved in the development of a gay, lesbian, or bisexual identity can help faculty create positive, inclusive learning environments.

D'Augelli's Model of Gay, Lesbian, and Bisexual Identity Development

Anthony D'Augelli (1994) viewed lesbian, gay, and bisexual identity development as a complex process involving multiple interacting factors that must be understood within context and historical time. Three sets of variables influence the development of a gay, lesbian, or bisexual identity: personal subjectivities and actions, interactive intimacies, and sociohistorical connections (D'Augelli, 1994). *Personal subjectivities and actions* are the ways in which individuals interpret their experiences and react to them emotionally and behaviorally. *Interactive intimacies* include interactions with significant others, including parents, family, and peers, that influence the development and interpretation of one's sexual behaviors and beliefs. *Sociohistorical connections* are the norms and expectations that exist in particular geographical locations or cultural groups, existing laws and policies, and the events and values of various historical time periods. These three variables interact in complex ways as individuals determine how they will present themselves in their daily lives.

D'Augelli (1994) argued that the development of sexual orientation is not a onetime event; rather, sexual and affectional feelings can change over the course of the life span. These feelings, and the degree to which the individual acts on them, are very much affected by changes in personal, family, and social expectations. D'Augelli stressed the plasticity of human functioning, noting that it is strongly influenced both by circumstances in the environment and by physical and biological changes experienced at different points over the life course. As a result, sexual identity can be very fluid at some times in a person's life and more solidified at others. For many students, the college years are a time of considerable fluidity because of changes in relationships with family caused by leaving home, new peer groups, and the new roles assumed in college. During periods of uncertainty and exploration, students are often anxious and preoccupied, factors that can interfere with the learning process (McMillan and Forsyth, 1991).

D'Augelli (1994) also stressed the uniqueness of individual development. No two individuals follow the same developmental path. However, the extent of variation will differ during certain periods in an individual's life, in certain types of families and communities, and in different historical periods. For instance, a student coming from a conservative family attending an evangelical Christian college in a rural community would appear to have fewer options with regard to expression of sexual identity than a student attending a large public university in a metropolitan area whose parents are active in social justice issues.

A final point that D'Augelli (1994) stressed was that individuals play an important role in their own development. Individuals make active choices that influence the people they become. Context does shape this process, however. Because our culture provides no systematic socialization for gay, lesbian, and bisexual people, they have to determine their own developmental path. Unfortunately, the negative forces of discrimination and victimization directed toward lesbian, gay, and bisexual people often create roadblocks to successful self-development for this population. And the struggle with identity development often compromises learning in other areas.

D'Augelli (1994) identified a number of intertwined processes involved in the development of a lesbian, gay, or bisexual identity. These processes are influenced by the cultural and interpersonal contexts in which they occur. The first process is *exiting a heterosexual identity*. This task involves coming to an understanding of one's attractions, labeling them, and exploring the implications of this awareness for one's life. In modern society, heterosexuality is assumed to be the norm, and from the time of their birth, individuals are taught to reject any characteristics that might indicate a homosexual orientation. As a result, coming to an awareness that one is not heterosexual and giving up the privileges and acceptance that come with a heterosexual identity are difficult and painful processes that take a significant amount of time. Exiting a heterosexual identity also involves telling other people that one is lesbian, gay, or bisexual. This "coming out" experience is not a one-time event but rather a process that must be renegotiated with each person to whom one chooses to disclose. Certainly disclosing to one's faculty and classmates, people who play a significant role in one's academic success, can be a difficult and anxiety-provoking experience. Often preoccupation over whether or not to come out supersedes paying attention to course content and interferes with learning that would otherwise take place.

Developing a personal lesbian, gay, or bisexual identity status is a process that must be simultaneously addressed while one is exiting a heterosexual identity. Because few positive role models exist for how to "be" gay, lesbian, or bisexual, establishing a new, nonheterosexual life is very difficult. Some contact with a lesbian, gay, or bisexual community is usually required during this process. Individuals must also come to an awareness of the myths and stereotypes they themselves hold about lesbian, gay, and bisexual people. A classroom environment in which lesbian, gay, and bisexual topics are discussed and students can be open about their identities provides opportunities for students to learn about what it really means to be lesbian, gay, and bisexual.

A third process lesbian, gay, and bisexual students must address is *developing a lesbian, gay, or bisexual social identity.* This process involves creating a social network of people who know and affirm one's sexual orientation. Since the reactions of others can never truly be known before an individual comes out, building and maintaining a support network is particularly challenging for a gay, lesbian, or bisexual individual. Because peer and faculty support are key factors in learning (Kuh, Douglas, Lund, and Ramin-Gyurnek, 1994), faculty need to be particularly attentive to creating conditions that help lesbian, gay, and bisexual students build affirming social networks.

Becoming a lesbian, gay, or bisexual offspring involves revealing one's sexual identity to one's parents and redefining one's relationship with them. In most cases, this process is stressful and requires significant work on the part of the lesbian, gay, or bisexual child (Savin-Williams, 1998b). Obviously, the potential for learning is adversely affected when students are struggling to gain parental acceptance of their sexual identity. As illustrated by the quote presented earlier, having faculty to whom one can turn at such times can be very helpful.

Developing a lesbian, gay, or bisexual intimacy status is a difficult process because of the lack of visible role models in our society. Often one's first significant intimate relationship is formed in college (Savin-Williams, 1998a). Students who are immersed in making an intimate relationship "work" may have trouble staying focused on classroom learning.

Entering a lesbian, gay, or bisexual community involves determining the extent to which one will be active politically. Some individuals will decide that their sexuality is strictly a private matter. Others, however, will feel an obligation to be politically active in order to address the inequities faced by all lesbian, gay, and bisexual people. Being an activist can be risky; one may experience harassment, discrimination, and even violence. Often lesbian, gay, and bisexual students first become involved in political activity in college. Faculty validation of students' efforts and acknowledgment of the risks can encourage students to make links between their in- and out-of-classroom learning experiences.

In summary, D'Augelli (1994) stated that identity is a "dynamic process of interaction and exchange between the individual and the many levels of social collectives during the historical period of his or her life" (p. 330). He also stressed the importance of acknowledging the significant influence of heterosexism, homophobia, and disenfranchisement on the lives of gay, lesbian, and bisexual individuals. Faculty can play an important role in addressing these issues in the classroom by actively acknowledging students' experiences and providing support at times of stress.

A Continuum of Classroom Experiences

As Tiberius and Billson (1991) pointed out, social context plays an important role in learning. Based on a qualitative study of the classroom experiences of lesbian, gay, and bisexual students, De Surra and Church (1994) developed a continuum of marginalization and centralization experiences. Connolly (1999) expanded their model and provided further examples. Following is a summary of the model, highlighting negative and positive influences the classroom context can have.

Explicit Marginalization. In classrooms where gay, lesbian, and bisexual students are explicitly marginalized, faculty or other students make homophobic statements that go unchallenged. Negative references may be made to the sexuality of historical figures, authors, or characters in literature, or incorrect information may be given concerning gay, lesbian, or bisexual people or issues. Explicit marginalization is also evident in the omission of material on lesbian, gay, or bisexual topics in courses that warrant their inclusion, such as courses in human sexuality.

In such a classroom, lesbian, gay, and bisexual students feel very uncomfortable and unwelcome. Some students, especially those who are more secure in their identity, will endure the negative environment in such a class by remaining silent. Struggling to overcome such hostility, however, is likely to interfere significantly with the students' ability to learn. Many lesbian, gay, and bisexual students will drop such a class or even leave school to escape the hostile environment.

Implicit Marginalization. Implicit marginalization consists of indirect and covert messages that gay, lesbian, and bisexual orientations are abnormal and not worthy of consideration except as examples illustrating deviance. While lesbian, gay, and bisexual individuals are not directly attacked, neither are lesbian, gay, or bisexual issues openly acknowledged. Heterosexist language and examples permeate discussion, and students are discouraged from discussing or independently pursuing topics related to sexual orientation.

Though students may feel less threatened than in a class that is explicitly marginalizing, they can also feel very much alone and discounted if they were to raise issues related to sexual orientation. As a result, they may disengage from the class and perform poorly.

Implicit Centralization. An implicitly centralized classroom provides a more welcoming environment for gay, lesbian, and bisexual students. In such classrooms, faculty confront homophobic or heterosexist comments when they are made by students. They may also point out heterosexist assumptions in course reading material or support gay, lesbian, or bisexual students' statements related to sexual orientation issues. Faculty do not, however, proactively address gay, lesbian, and bisexual topics in course content or instructional strategies.

In an implicitly centralized classroom, gay, lesbian, and bisexual students are often surprised and grateful when they experience support for their positions. They are likely to feel more a part of such a class and to participate more actively than in nonsupportive classrooms, thereby increasing the potential for learning.

Explicit Centralization. In explicitly centralized classrooms, faculty actively support gay, lesbian, and bisexual students by intentionally including material on gay, lesbian, and bisexual topics. Language and examples used in class are inclusive. Faculty create and model a climate in which all perspectives are heard and valued.

Because such classes are rare, gay, lesbian, and bisexual students who are looking for opportunities to learn more about lesbian, gay, and bisexual topics eagerly seek them out. Such classes provide "safe spaces" for students where they can openly address issues, explore topics of interest to them, and most important of all, be themselves. Great potential for learning exists for all students in such classes.

Conclusion

So what does sexual orientation have to do with learning in the classroom? Resolving the developmental processes involved in establishing one's sexual orientation can interfere with the learning that normally occurs in the classroom. For learning to occur unimpeded, students must feel that they are safe, valued, and supported. Faculty can create such a climate by creating centralized classrooms in which gay, lesbian, and bisexual issues are routinely addressed.

And how can unnecessary controversy and irrelevant discussion be avoided when sexual orientation is addressed in the classroom? Faculty play an important role in establishing positive classroom norms. Adding a statement of nondiscrimination and appreciation of diversity to one's syllabus and underscoring these values during the first class meeting sets a positive tone for the class. Immediately confronting any insensitive remarks demonstrates that faculty members indeed mean what they initially stated.

Finally, what if your field is chemistry? In any field, the classroom atmosphere affects lesbian, gay, and bisexual students. Icy stares from peers or inappropriate language used by lab partners can interfere with learning. By contrast, a nondiscrimination statement on a syllabus or a Safe Zone sticker on an office door sends a message of support that allows a student to focus on chemistry rather than fending off a hostile classroom climate.

References

Connolly, M. "Issues for Lesbian, Gay, and Bisexual Students in Traditional College Classrooms." In V. A. Wall and N. J. Evans (eds.), *Toward Acceptance: Sexual Orientation Issues on Campus.* Lanham, Md.: American College Personnel Association, 1999.

D'Augelli, A. R. "Identity Development and Sexual Orientation: Toward a Model of Lesbian, Gay, and Bisexual Development." In E. J. Trickett, R. J. Watts, and D. Birman (eds.), *Human Diversity: Perspectives on People in Context.* San Francisco: Jossey-Bass, 1994.

De Surra, C. J., and Church, C. A. "Unlocking the Classroom Closet: Privileging the Marginalized Voices of Gay/Lesbian College Students." Paper presented at the annual meeting of the Speech Communication Association, New Orleans, Nov. 1994.

Evans, N. J. "Safe Zone Evaluation: Preliminary Analysis." [http://www.public.iastate.edu/~clund/safezones]. 1998.

Kuh, G. D., Douglas, K. B., Lund, J. P., and Ramin-Gyurnek, J. *Student Learning Outside the Classroom: Transcending Artificial Boundaries.* ASHE-ERIC Higher Education Report, no. 8. Washington, D.C.: School of Education and Human Development, George Washington University, 1994.

McMillan, J. H., and Forsyth, D. R. "What Theories of Motivation Say About Why Learners Learn." In R. J. Menges and M. D. Svinicki (eds.), *College Teaching: From Theory to Practice.* New Directions for Teaching and Learning, no. 45. San Francisco: Jossey-Bass, 1991.

Rendón, L. I. "Validating Culturally Diverse Students: Toward a New Model of Learning and Student Development." *Innovative Higher Education,* 1994, *19,* 33–51.

Savin-Williams, R. C. ". . . And Then I Became Gay": Young Men's Stories.* New York: Routledge, 1998a.

Savin-Williams, R. C. "Lesbian, Gay, and Bisexual Youths' Relationships with Their Parents." In C. J. Patterson and A. R. D'Augelli (eds.), *Lesbian, Gay, and Bisexual Identities in Families: Psychological Perspectives.* New York: Oxford University Press, 1998b.

Tiberius, R. G., and Billson, J. M. "The Social Context of Teaching and Learning." In R. J. Menges and M. D. Svinicki (eds.), *College Teaching: From Theory to Practice.* New Directions for Teaching and Learning, no. 45. San Francisco: Jossey-Bass, 1991.

NANCY J. EVANS is an associate professor in the Department of Educational Leadership and Policy Studies at Iowa State University in Ames.

9

*Longitudinal data on young adults' learning and
development integrate the multiple dimensions of
development described throughout this volume.
Chapter authors' recommendations are synthesized
to guide faculty in understanding and using students'
meaning-making to enhance learning.*

Teaching to Promote Holistic Learning and Development

Marcia B. Baxter Magolda

The authors in this volume clarify that the learning expectations we have
for college students require complex intrapersonal, interpersonal, and cognitive levels of development. The student stories in each chapter illustrate
the more typical ways in which college students make meaning and their
journeys toward the more complex ways of making meaning we hope they
will achieve during college. Higher education has been clear about the
desired destination of this journey, or the nature of Ignelzi's metaphorical
farm, that we want students to inhabit; educators have been less clear about
the farms on which students currently live and how to map the journey
from one to the other. The intent of this volume is to bring students' farms
to life for educators and to guide educators in offering students maps and
company to reach new farms.

The first eight chapters explore various dimensions and facets of development in-depth and with particular groups of students to deepen understanding of the multiple ways in which college-age adults interpret their
experience and thus how they learn. This chapter integrates these dimensions and facets of development to emphasize a holistic perspective of student development and learning. I draw on stories from my fourteen-year
longitudinal study of young adults' meaning-making to form a holistic view
of learning. I also synthesize the authors' recommendations for accessing
students' meaning-making and creating inclusive, effective learning environments for all students.

New Directions for Teaching and Learning, no. 82, Summer 2000 © Jossey-Bass Publishers

A Holistic View of Learning and Development

Following young adults longitudinally through annual in-depth qualitative interviews (Baxter Magolda, 1992, 1999c) afforded me an opportunity to see the multiple dimensions and facets of development discussed in this volume integrated in each young adult's life. Because our interviews span from the first year of college to the participants' early thirties, the transition from meaning-making typical in college to more complex forms is evident in their stories.

Alice is a counselor in a social service agency. An interview she gave in her junior year reveals the cognitive, intrapersonal, and interpersonal meaning-making described as typical of many college students in the preceding chapters. Like most of her peers in the study, Alice was defined through what others expected of her. Her cognitive meaning-making is evident in this comment: "I've noticed that a lot of things professors say are opinion, and it's their own experience. It has to be because it's not real factual material. If it is a definite fact or statistic or a definition, they'll say. I think that's good in a lot of ways, though, because it makes me think, 'What have I ever done that fits into this?' If one made more sense to me personally, that's probably the way I would go with it." Alice ascertained that this change had to do with subject matter, saying, "In a calculus class it's not so much opinion oriented. It's like it's right or it's wrong; these are the facts." In her family studies classes, however, she reported that "there are no facts. You just go on theories and studies mixed in with them" (Baxter Magolda, 1992, p. 115).

Alice's thinking illustrates what I called *transitional knowing,* characterized by the assumption that truth exists in some areas (calculus, for example) whereas uncertainty reigns in others (say, family studies). Alice relies on her personal feelings to decide what to believe in the uncertain areas, much like Clinchy's subjectivists in Chapter Three and King's quasi-reflective thinkers in Chapter Two. Alice is just beginning to encounter the notion of thinking for herself; she does not yet have an internal sense of self to guide her choices. This is evident in her explanation of choices during college. For example, Alice described how she decided to join a sorority: "I rushed, and then I just ended up liking it. I'm pretty involved in it. There's no real explanation for why. That's just the way it happened." She seemed to make decisions about involvement in sorority activities versus her academic work in much the same way: "Monday night we ended up having a party and I should have stayed home and read. But I went anyway. There's a lot more to school than just getting your chapters read. It's really hard to strike a happy medium. I don't really know that I even have a happy medium of it." Like most of her peers in the study, Alice's decisions during college reflected her fusion with others' expectations of her, reflective of Kegan's third order of consciousness (1994; see also Chapter One). She seems unsure of what she wants and goes with the flow of what others around her are doing.

Alice did report feeling more open-minded as a junior than she had as a freshman. She explained that people she knew in her small town were pretty much the same, saying, "There were only two Catholic families in my hometown. I just felt completely naive and stupid [about their faith]. I had to have my roommate explain to me what all these things mean. And with stuff like that, naturally you're saying that if it's not familiar, . . . it's bad. Freshman year I probably even did because I was probably pretty sheltered. But now it's just like whatever, your opinion. Just because people have a different opinion doesn't mean that you have to disagree about a lot of things." Alice articulates Ortiz's link between cultural identity and worldview (see Chapter Seven) in her realization that what she has grown up with as familiar she saw as right. Alice is at the beginning of Ortiz's concept of intercultural competence as she begins to recognize the validity of other perspectives. However, as a subjective, transitional, quasi-reflective thinker, she has no mechanism for analyzing these new perspectives. She has yet to explore her own cultural or racial identity in any depth, in part because she has not explored her own identity in general.

It was not until graduate school, which Alice started in her mid-twenties, that she began the transition to more complex cognitive, intrapersonal, and interpersonal ways of making meaning (Baxter Magolda, 1998). She reported the effect of taking a multicultural education class: "It's made me real conscious of my own assumptions and my own frame of reference, realizing that it is my own frame of reference, but it doesn't mean I have to be locked inside of it. I can't get away from my own feelings and biases, but I can be aware of [them] and work with [them] and around [them]." This class offered Alice an encounter similar to the kind Howard-Hamilton (Chapter Five) and Ortiz (Chapter Seven) described as the impetus for racial and cultural identity development. Alice's initial awareness of her whiteness began the process of her own cultural identity development. Her awareness of her own sense of self was also emerging, as she described her counseling work: "I try to sugar-coat things. And that's something that I do need to look at because it's not doing the clients any favors. They need the honest truth. And it's my hang-up that's sugar-coating it. I'm not doing it for their benefit; I'm doing it for mine. That's been probably the most valuable thing with the hands-on stuff with clients is that I'm realizing what my own issues are." Alice is starting to differentiate between what she does for her own needs and what she does for others, illustrative of the transition between Kegan's third and fourth orders. She sees the need for making up her own mind or becoming a reflective thinker:

> I'm finding that I'm really questioning things and issues. I'm really sorting stuff out for myself instead of just taking notes about everybody else's opinion. Hands-on experience made me realize nobody else is in this room with me when I'm doing this counseling session. To be clear on these issues, I need to figure them out for myself. Not to say that I'm ever going to figure them out, but to know where I stand on them and to think them through. I feel like if I'm not sure where I stand or I'm not clear on what the issues are and what

the arguments are both ways and process that myself, then I don't see how I can be of any help at all to this client.

Alice realizes that she must be clear on issues herself in order to help her clients and that she must separate her issues from theirs. She is progressing toward an internal sense of self. She is also progressing toward Rhoads's caring self (see Chapter Four) in her concern for the well-being of her clients.

By her early thirties, Alice had learned how to process things herself and achieved an internal sense of self that guided her decisions about what to believe and how to conduct herself professionally and personally. Having experienced a change of heart that led her to change her work role to accommodate parenting her children, she commented: "It really wasn't a struggle. It was a matter of 'Wow, I never thought I'd feel this way.' I certainly respected people who did think this way, but I just didn't think I would. But it wasn't like I was trying to change my mind. It was 'Now I have these feelings, I know what they are; I trust that; now what do I do about it?'" (Baxter Magolda, 1999a, p. 640).

In describing how she figured out what to do about it, Alice exhibited the double vision of connection and separation Clinchy noted in Chapter Three as essential for complex knowing:

> I think there has always been a rational component. But ultimately it has to feel right in the gut. My main approach as a counselor is a strong cognitive, rational piece to my therapy. I constantly tell clients just because we feel a certain way doesn't mean we have to act on it. There is a rational process that needs to be there—I didn't quit my job the first day I had this feeling! But I have always had access to that gut awareness and probably some of that is spiritual. My prayer life and spiritual life has always been there. That is very interrelated to that gut feeling—what is the right thing for me? I don't act immediately on this gut feeling, I sort through that with rational processes "Why do I feel this way?" and "What does it mean financially?" And "How can I prepare to do that in a way that is responsible to other people?" I have chosen to take on responsibility, and there are lots of people who trust the decisions I am going to make. Knowing that, respecting that, I'm not going to rush—there is going to be a transition period, room to explore how all this fits and how do we make this smooth. I guess the gut leads me and the rational thinking sorts out the details" (Baxter Magolda, 1999a, p. 640).

Alice's cognitive development, evident in her decision-making process, reflects Clinchy's constructed knower and King's reflective thinker. I called this way of knowing contextual because participants decided what to believe in context (Baxter Magolda, 1992). As King and Howard-Hamilton (1999) and Ortiz (Chapter Seven) noted, this complex level of reasoning is related to multicultural or intercultural competence. The ability to take perspectives outside one's own and the ability to reflect on one's own perspective critically lead to respect and appreciation of other views, much as Alice respected people who valued motherhood over career aspirations even before she came to that perspective. She also gained appreciation for the varying cultural perspectives of her clients. This perspective taking is related to Rhoads's caring self in Alice's concern for others who would be affected by her decision and her responsibility toward their well-being in the transition.

Closely related to these complex levels of cognitive and intrapersonal development is Alice's interpersonal complexity, evident in this comment:

> I'll be honest: one of the things that went through my mind was what will other people think about this decision? A lot of professional contacts I've made . . . see me as career oriented and competent, and I think those things are true and complementary, and I just wonder what their reactions will be. Will they be supportive? Will they understand? If they don't, it doesn't change my choice, but I've wondered. I'm not immune from that. It doesn't take priority over what is inside. I guess I don't need that acceptance or approval—[though] I'd like it—to know that I am doing the right thing.

Alice makes it clear that she would like approval from others but doesn't need it to know she is doing the right thing. The fact that what is inside takes priority reveals that Alice's internal sense of self has solidified to the point that she is no longer constructed by others' expectations—she has reached Kegan's fourth order. Yet she is still connected to other people, and her caring self ensures that she balances her needs with those of her family and coworkers.

Alice's journey from external to internal self-definition mirrors the journeys related in the first eight chapters despite variations in dynamics Alice did not experience (such as sexual orientation or African American racial status). However, as Evans pointed out in Chapter Eight, coming out as a gay, lesbian, or bisexual person requires affirming one's sense of self separate from what others expect—a characteristic of Kegan's fourth order, an internal sense of identity, and the ability to author one's own views. Similarly, Howard-Hamilton in Chapter Five and Fries-Britt in Chapter Six indicate that support from one's cultural peers (perhaps a third-order concept) gives one the strength to affirm one's racial identity regardless of racism in the environment. The complex stages of racial identity reflect the complex intrapersonal and interpersonal dimensions of Kegan's fourth order as well as the complex cognitive dimension evident in reflective or constructed thinking. Thus while gay, lesbian, or bisexual students and students of color have additional layers of identity development to address, the underlying journey remains one of moving from external to internal self-definition and authority.

Helping students along this difficult journey can help them address multiple dimensions of their development that mediate their ability to meet the learning expectations they face in college. Helping students map this journey may seem like a daunting task, particularly in light of Alice's arrival at complex functioning in her early thirties, a situation typical of most of her peers. However, the chapter authors have provided multiple possibilities for understanding students' development and promoting their learning. It is to this task we turn next.

Accessing Students' Meaning-Making

Educators cannot possibly know the backgrounds, unique experiences, and developmental journeys of every student they encounter. Recognizing, however, that these backgrounds, unique experiences, and developmental journeys mediate learning necessitates finding ways to access students' meaning-making to promote learning more effectively. In Chapter Seven, Ortiz sketches the characteristics of intercultural competence, including the ability to see things from different perspectives, moving outside one's own frame of reference, respect of people's background, and an interest in learning more about people—their culture and history. As educators interact with increasingly diverse students, Ortiz's concept of intercultural competence becomes central to creating effective teaching and learning environments. If we are to understand our students, we need to visit their farms and express genuine interest in learning about their experiences. The recommendations in the first eight chapters regarding accessing students' meaning-making all center on listening carefully to how students make meaning of their experience.

Ignelzi demonstrated in Chapter One that young adults can articulate their expectations and needs in a supervisory context. From this observation, he argued that faculty could ask for and listen to students' expectations in the teacher-student relationship. Hearing students' views of the role of the teacher, the kind of support they hope to receive, and the type of guidance they need gives the faculty member clues to their meaning-making processes. Similarly, the questions in King's examples of varying levels of reflective thinking in Chapter Two are questions that can be integrated into class discussion. Hearing students' assumptions about the nature of knowledge and the justification of beliefs reveal their progress toward reflective thinking. Asking students to discuss their approach to controversial material would elicit the dynamics Clinchy outlined in Chapter Three regarding connection and separation, as well as various ways of knowing. My longitudinal participants readily described the role of instructors, peers, and themselves in the contexts in which they learned best (Baxter Magolda, 1992). Engaging students in these dialogues at the outset of a course as well as during a course as appropriate could help faculty sense how students are making meaning to understand how this will mediate learning in the course.

Authors of the chapters focused on identity development also advocate listening to students to understand the multiple layers of their identity development. Evans's emphasis in Chapter Eight on expressing one's role as an ally is crucial here. Her notion of an ally in the context of gay, lesbian, and bisexual students' experience is in fact important to all students. Often students sense that their personal struggles are irrelevant to educators or simply perceived as excuses for their difficulties in academic work. Thus they hesitate to share their internal conflicts; this hesitation is heightened when they are unsure of an educator's stance on race or sexual orientation. Howard-Hamilton's example in Chapter Five of the white teacher's racial identity development shows how the teacher's perspective can affect students' willingness to share their thoughts. Fries-Britt's data in Chapter Six underscore the importance of faculty's welcoming students' concerns about race or gender as well as constructing relationships based on mutual respect. Expressing openness to learning about and respecting students' experiences can create opportunities to hear how their unique experiences affect their learning.

Rhoads's discussion of service learning in Chapter Four offers yet another avenue to access students' meaning-making. Direct experience coupled with reflection helped students develop a caring self. The notion of direct experience can be incorporated into classroom activities, accompanied by intentional opportunities for reflection that reveal students' meaning-making. Making reflection a part of the learning environment also conveys to students that educators are interested in how they make sense of their experience. This process welcomes students as they are and are becoming, similar to Ignelzi's recommendation that we simultaneously welcome and facilitate development. Such facilitation helps us create inclusive and effective learning environments.

Creating Inclusive and Effective Learning Environments

Inclusive and effective learning environments as defined in this volume are environments in which opportunities for complex cognitive, intrapersonal, and interpersonal development exist for all students. The multitude of recommendations in the first eight chapters can be organized into four main themes: viewing students as capable participants in the journey to self-authorship, providing directions and practice in acquiring internal authority, establishing communities of learners among peers, and supporting the struggle inherent in exchanging older, simpler perspectives for newer, more complex ones.

Viewing Students as Capable Participants in the Journey to Self-Authorship. This involves valuing and respecting students' experience and current development. This theme is evident in the authors' recommendations for accessing students' meaning-making, as already discussed. The recommendations highlight two primary arenas in which this respect is conveyed in the classroom. First, educators' attitude toward students must convey respect. King suggests that respecting and providing support for students' current meaning-making helps them take the risks required to move to more complex ways of making meaning. My study participants reported that they were able to move toward self-authorship when they were validated as capable of knowing (Baxter Magolda, 1992). Ignelzi explains that showing that "we understand how it is for them" creates the interpersonal connection needed by third-order students to feel supported. Rhoads's notion of mutuality, or situating all parties as "givers" and "receivers," is another way of conveying support to externally defined students. Finally, showing respect for students' race, ethnicity, culture, and sexual orientation welcomes important aspects of their experience in the learning endeavor. Fries-Britt's emphasis on affirmation of black students, Ortiz's suggestions for including cultural issues in the dialogue, Howard-Hamilton's encouragement of self-exploration, and Evans's safe zone are all versions of this welcoming dynamic.

Second, respect for students' experience is conveyed through the curriculum and course syllabus. Evans's recommendation for a centralized curriculum in which issues of sexual orientation are openly addressed when appropriate in one example of a welcoming attitude in action. Howard-Hamilton's explanation of the transformed course, in which traditional assumptions are questioned and transformed in light of multiple perspectives, is another example of welcoming diverse students' experience by incorporating material relevant to race, ethnicity, and culture into the course of study. The theme of respecting students and their experience is also interwoven throughout the three remaining themes.

Providing Directions and Practice in Acquiring Internal Authority. Ignelzi advocates offering students good directions to the new farm and accompanying them on the journey there. His call for structured, supervised practice in generating one's own ideas about course material is answered by numerous chapter authors' recommendations addressing the nature of class activities, evaluation, and the role of the teacher. King offers a comprehensive view of classroom activities that center around teaching students strategies for gathering and evaluating data in order to make interpretive judgments. She advocates using controversial, ill-structured issues that explicitly contain uncertainty in judgment to help students explore lines of reasoning. Similarly, Howard-Hamilton advocates exercises in perspective taking. Ortiz recommends dialogue on complex topics to help students attend to multiple perspectives and expand their understanding. King also emphasizes opportunities for students to analyze others' views and to defend their own. Rhoads's emphasis on personalizing learning interactions followed by intentional reflection supports students' opportunities to analyze their own and others' views. Clinchy notes that inviting students to say what they really think and using their ideas as hypotheses for exploration helps them develop their thoughts. I found this to be true among my study participants as well as students in classes I observed (Baxter Magolda, 1999b). These approaches support Ortiz's call for community building to allow risk taking and using collaborative and active learning methods.

These approaches focus on eliciting students' thinking, engaging them in reflection and analysis, and guiding them in reorganizing their thinking in more complex ways. The same process can be implemented in evaluating students' work. Ortiz advocates assignments that require complex thinking by integrating critical analysis of the subject matter and students' experience, thus giving students experience in the kind of meaning-making we hope they will achieve. Giving students frequent feedback on such work provides both cognitive and emotional support for their efforts, according to King. Clinchy and Fries-Britt emphasize affirmation of the student in concert with constructive criticism. Fries-Britt explains that affirming the positive aspects of students' work affirms their sense of self, making them more able to accept constructive criticism. Likewise, Clinchy advocates that helping students connect to their work via its positive characteristics affirms connection before taking a detached stance to critique one's ideas. She also notes that connected education requires a more personal, noncompetitive approach to evaluation to engender the students' investment in their work. These notions convey the balance of welcoming students as they are while inviting them to become something more.

Finally, the role the educator adopts can offer direction and good company for the journey to internal authority. Clinchy speaks most directly to the educator's role in modeling complex ways of making meaning. She advocates that educators share the process (rather than only the product) of their own thinking by thinking out loud and being willing to change their minds in classroom dialogue. Doing so reflects what Howard-Hamilton called collaboration, which helps students understand the creation of meaning. This role invites students to be partners in the learning process, just as Rhoads invited students to be partners in deciding the nature of service learning activities. This partnership is particularly important to students who have experienced marginalization, as illustrated in Fries-Britt's students' comments in Chapter Six that quality relationships with faculty enhanced their sense of intellectual capability. The process of mutually constructing meaning is also a key characteristic in helping students in various disciplines learn self-authorship (Baxter Magolda, 1992, 1999b) because they are guided in developing their own thinking by the educator's expertise.

Establishing Communities of Learners Among Peers. Despite the significance of the curriculum, educators' welcoming approach, and classroom formats that guide students effectively toward self-authorship, there is still a need for support among peers to learn effectively. Ignelzi notes that group work is essential to support third-order students who make meaning of their experience through those around them. The chapter authors show that communities of learners provide both the affirmation externally defined students need and the challenge to move them toward internal definition. Fries-Britt and Howard-Hamilton report that African American students flourished when they had strong peer support. Fries-Britt noted that students of color are often dispersed among groups to provide diversity in each group, often to their own detriment; she addressed the advantages of groups of students of color to provide affirmation. Evans's plans for achieving an environment of inclusiveness, not just by welcoming diversity but also by confronting insensitive remarks, also create an affirming peer community. King acknowledges the importance of peer communities in her recommendation that students be encouraged to practice their reasoning skills in student organizations and other settings to increase their confidence.

The authors also highlight the challenges peers offer each other. Ignelzi clarifies that any student group typically contains a range of meaning-making such that externally defined students are challenged by internally defined students. Clinchy suggests that students should have opportunities to get into the perspectives of their classmates and to think with them (connection) and against them (separation) to develop their own thoughts. Ortiz and Howard-Hamilton emphasize the value of multiple perspectives arising from group work. The processing of service learning experiences Rhoads advocates is another form of peers helping one another analyze their thoughts and develop perspectives. Organizing peer communities around the same mutuality and advancing the notion of partnership in the educator-student relationship create opportunities for risk taking, affirmation, challenge, and growth.

Supporting the Struggle Inherent in the Journey. Exchanging older, simpler perspectives for newer, more complex ones is not an easy process. William Perry (1970) likened it to the nostalgia of leaving one's current home, despite excitement about a new home. We do not easily let go of ways of understanding the world and ourselves that have been long in the making and that are more comfortable than newer ways that are not entirely clear to us yet. Moving from external definition means leaving the safety of having one's beliefs and identity defined by others to the responsibility of making those choices oneself. Remaking how one constructs knowledge, one's own identity, and one's relationships with others are all inherent in this journey. Thus Ignelzi's recommendation of standing by students during transitions is crucial. If we expect them to achieve the complex levels of meaning-making that advanced learning requires, we must acknowledge the struggle involved. Welcoming students' reflections during the journey conveys understanding and empathy for these important tasks.

Conclusion

The possible ways students make meaning sketched throughout this volume reveal how meaning-making in cognitive, intrapersonal, and interpersonal dimensions mediates learning. The authors' proposals for accessing their students' meaning-making and creating inclusive and effective learning environments demonstrate that teaching can simultaneously meet learning goals and promote self-authorship. The authors' insights expand on contemporary teaching approaches such as constructivist teaching (for example, Twomey Fosnot, 1996; von Glasersfeld, 1995), collaborative learning (Bruffee, 1993), caring education (Noddings, 1991), empowering education (Shor, 1992), feminist teaching (Maher and Tetreault, 1994), and culturally relevant pedagogy (Ladson-Billings, 1995) by emphasizing the developmental progression of students' meaning-making.

The holistic view of learning and development advanced here does, however, require new assumptions about knowledge, authority, learners, and teachers. Guiding students to author their own knowledge in the context of existing knowledge recognizes that knowledge is socially constructed by knowledgeable peers. As a result, authority is transformed from providing knowledge to assisting in its construction. Assuming that students are in the process of learning to construct knowledge, teachers join them as partners in the knowledge construction process. It is in joining students as partners that educators gain access to their meaning-making and the opportunity to map the pathways to self-authorship from particular students' starting points on the journey.

References

Baxter Magolda, M. B. *Knowing and Reasoning in College: Gender-Related Patterns in Students' Intellectual Development.* San Francisco: Jossey-Bass, 1992.

Baxter Magolda, M. B. "Developing Self-Authorship in Graduate School." In M. A. Anderson (ed.), *The Experience of Being in Graduate School: An Exploration.* New Directions for Higher Education, no. 101. San Francisco: Jossey-Bass, 1998.

Baxter Magolda, M. B. "Constructing Adult Identities." *Journal of College Student Development,* 1999a, *40,* 629–644.

Baxter Magolda, M. B. *Creating Contexts for Learning and Self-Authorship: Constructive-Developmental Pedagogy.* Nashville, Tenn.: Vanderbilt University Press, 1999b.

Baxter Magolda, M. B. "The Evolution of Epistemology: Refining Contextual Knowing at Twentysomething." *Journal of College Student Development,* 1999c, *40,* 333–344.

Bruffee, K. A. *Collaborative Learning: Higher Education, Interdependence, and the Authority of Knowledge.* Baltimore: Johns Hopkins University Press, 1993.

Kegan, R. *In over Our Heads: The Mental Demands of Modern Life.* Cambridge, Mass.: Harvard University Press, 1994.

King, P. M., and Howard-Hamilton, M. F. "Becoming a Multiculturally Competent Student Affairs Professional." Final report submitted to the National Association of Student Personnel Administrators, 1999. Available from Patricia King, School of Leadership and Policy Studies, Bowling Green State University, Bowling Green, OH 43403.

Ladson-Billings, G. "Toward a Theory of Culturally Relevant Pedagogy." *American Educational Research Journal,* 1995, *32,* 465–491.

Maher, F. A., and Tetreault, M. K. *The Feminist Classroom: An Inside Look at How Professors and Students Are Transforming Higher Education for a Diverse Society.* New York: Basic Books, 1994.

Noddings, N. "Stories in Dialogue: Caring and Interpersonal Reasoning." In C. Witherell and N. Noddings (eds.), *Stories Lives Tell: Narrative and Dialogue in Education.* New York: Teachers College Press, 1991.

Perry, W. G., Jr. *Forms of Intellectual and Ethical Development in the College Years: A Scheme.* Austin, Tex.: Holt, Rinehart and Winston, 1970.

Shor, I. *Empowering Education: Critical Teaching for Social Change.* Chicago: University of Chicago Press, 1992.

Twomey Fosnot, C. (ed.). *Constructivism: Theory, Perspectives, and Practice.* New York: Teachers College Press, 1996.

von Glasersfeld, E. "A Constructivist Approach to Teaching." In L. P. Steffe and J. Gale (eds.), *Constructivism in Education.* Mahwah, N.J.: Erlbaum, 1995.

MARCIA B. BAXTER MAGOLDA *is professor of educational leadership at Miami University, Oxford, Ohio.*

INDEX

Ability: blending of racial identity and, 55–65; concealing of, in high-ability black collegians, 57–58; level of meaning-making versus, 10–11; need to prove, in high-ability black collegians, 58–59

Academic concentration, choice of, 29–30

Acculturation, 70; in college, 70–72; dimensions of, 70; levels of, 70

"Acting white," 57

Active learning methods, 77, 97

Adversarial reasoning, 30–31

Affective or spiritual acculturation, 70

Affirmation, 13–14, 97

African American history and culture, learning about, 47–48, 70, 71–72

African American students, 45–54; culturally responsive learning environments for, 45, 50–52; faculty interaction with, 62–63, 64; high-ability, 55–65; like-type learning communities for, 64, 96–97; literature review of, 55; peer support for, 57, 59–62, 64, 93, 96–97; racial identity theories and, 45–49, 71–72. See also High-ability black collegians

Alienation, detachment and, 27–28

Allen, W. R., 55, 62, 65

American culture and worldview, 74

Aristotelian view of governance, 37

Asian Americans, 70

Assessment: blind grading for, 31; of class, 52; of connected knowing, 34; of meaning-making order, 11–12; of separate knowing, 34; of students' meaning-making, 93–94; to support holistic development, 96

Assimilated level of acculturation, 70

Association of American Colleges, 23, 25

Atkinson, D. R., 70, 78

Authorities, 28–29

Authority figures, high-ability black collegians and, 57–58

Autonomy status, 49, 50

Awareness stage of racial identity, 47

Banking education, 46, 51

Base groups, 77

Baxter Magolda, M. B., 1–3, 7, 10, 14, 23, 24, 25, 41, 44, 74, 78, 88, 89, 90, 91, 92, 95, 96, 98

Behavioral acculturation, 70

Belenky, M. F., 28, 34

Beliefs, justification of. See Justification of beliefs

Believing game, 31–32

Bellah, R. N., 38, 44

Benson, L., 38, 44

Berryhill-Paapke, E., 70, 78

Bicultural level of acculturation, 70

Billson, J. M., 82, 85, 87

Bisexual students. See Gay, lesbian, and bisexual students

Bleich, D., 31, 34

Blind grading, 31

Blumer, H., 40, 44

Brett, B., 29, 35

Bruffee, K. A., 98

Campus barriers to African American students, 56

Caring education, 99

Caring self, 37–44; defined, 37; democracy and, 38–39; in example, 92, 93; rationale and need for, 41–42; service learning for development of, 41–44, 95; social self and, 39–40

Casas, J. M., 70, 78

Case study analyses and discussions, 51, 77

Centralization of classroom, 86, 95

Certainty of knowledge: in prereflective thinking, 17, 20; in quasi-reflective thinking, 17, 20; in Reflective Judgment Model stages, summarized, 20–21; in reflective thinking, 18, 21, 22

Choney, S. K., 70, 78

Church, C. A., 85, 87

Classroom: addressing sexual orientation in, 85–87; centralization of, 86, 95; community-building in, 76–77; creating inclusive and effective, 94–97; developing intercultural competence in, 76–78; expressing cultural identity in, 67–79; gay, lesbian, and bisexual students in, continuum of experience in, 85–86; marginalization in, 85–86, 96. See also Learning environments

Clinchy, B. M., 2–3, 27, 28, 33, 34, 35, 89, 91, 93, 95, 96, 97

Co-construction of meaning. See Order 3 of meaning-making

Cognition, 1, 16. See also Epistemological dimension

Cognitive acculturation, 70

Cognitive development, worldviews and, 74. See also Epistemological dimension

Collaborative learning methods, 77, 96, 98

Coming out, 83–84, 92

Communities of learners, 96–97

Community: building, in the classroom, 76–77, 96–97; democracy and, 38–39; gay, lesbian, and bisexual, 84–85

Community service learning. See Service learning

Complex stage model, 19

Conformity stage of racial identity, 47

Connected education, 33–34

Connected knowing, 27–35; assessment of, 34; constructed knowing and, 32–33, 91–92; defined, 31–32; detachment versus, 27–28, 32, 34; separate knowing and, 32–33, 91, 93

Connolly, M., 85, 87

Constructed knowing, 32–33, 91–92. See also Connected knowing; Meaning-making

Back Issue/Subscription Order Form

Copy or detach and send to:
Jossey-Bass Publishers, 350 Sansome Street, San Francisco CA 94104-1342

Call or fax toll free!
Phone 888-378-2537 6AM-5PM PST; Fax 800-605-2665

Back issues: Please send me the following issues at $23 each
(Important: please include series initials and issue number, such as TL90)

1. TL _____

_____

_____

$ _____ Total for single issues

$ _____ Shipping charges (for single issues *only;* subscriptions are exempt
from shipping charges): Up to $30, add $5^{50} • $30^{01}–$50, add $6^{50}
$50^{01}–$75, add $8 • $75^{01}–$100, add $10 • $100^{01}–$150, add $12
Over $150, call for shipping charge

Subscriptions   Please ❑ start   ❑ renew my subscription to *New Directions for
Teaching and Learning* for the year _____ at the following rate:

U.S.:   ❑ Individual $58   ❑ Institutional $104
Canada: ❑ Individual $83   ❑ Institutional $129
All Others: ❑ Individual $88   ❑ Institutional $134
NOTE: Subscriptions are quarterly, and are for the calendar year only.
Subscriptions begin with the Spring issue of the year indicated above.

$ _____ Total single issues and subscriptions (Add appropriate sales tax
for your state for single issue orders. No sales tax for U.S. subscriptions.
Canadian residents, add GST for subscriptions and single issues.)

❑ Payment enclosed (U.S. check or money order only)
❑ VISA, MC, AmEx, Discover Card #_____ Exp. date_____

Signature _____ Day phone _____
❑ Bill me (U.S. institutional orders only. Purchase order required)
Purchase order #_____
Federal Tax ID 135593032   GST 89102-8052

Name _____

Address _____

_____

Phone_____ E-mail _____

For more information about Jossey-Bass Publishers, visit our Web site at:
www.josseybass.com   **PRIORITY CODE = ND1**

Printed in the United States
208656BV00002B/379-393/A